Musings of a Schizophrenic Drunk

I0103334

Amara Lorch

chipmunkapublishing
the mental health publisher

Amara Lorch

Published by
Chipmunkapublishing
PO Box 6872
Brentwood
Essex CM13 1ZT
United Kingdom

http://www.chipmunkapublishing.com

ISBN   978-1-84991-635-6

Chipmunkapublishing   gratefully   acknowledge   the support of Arts Council England.

Dedication

This book is dedicated to my best friend Phil
for his love and help
pulling me out of pain

Would you climb a tree with me? That would help. We could climb a rainforest giant and search for new kinds of bugs in the canopy. When we get so high that we are tired and the view is real nice, we will rest. The sounds will be deafening. So many birds and bugs competing for mates that conversation will be impossible. That's o.k. 'cause what is there to say anyway? We will look around and search for a larger tree with a fuller canopy; climb down and up again until we reach the sea. That would help.

Amara Lorch

Excerpt from Psalm 39
Of the Holy Bible

PSALM 39

I I said, "I will guard my ways, lest I sin with my tongue; I will restrain my mouth with a muzzle, while the wicked are before me."

2 I was mute with silence, I held my peace even from good; and my sorrow was stirred up.

3 My heart was hot within me; while I was musing, the fire burned. *Then* I spoke with my tongue:

4 "Lord, make me to know my end, and what *is* the measure of my days, *that* I may know how frail I am.

5 Indeed, You have made my days as handbreadths, and my age is as nothing before You; certainly every man at his best state *is* but vapor.

Selah

Author Biography

Amara grew up in the mountains of Colorado, competed nationally and internationally as an alpine ski racer, lived in the Ozark and Blue Ridge mountains, and now is a licensed arborist in Fort Collins, CO. Long days of hiking, biking, gardening, climbing trees, skiing, and relaxing by river banks leave images printed on her mind. In her writing and artwork, she shares these memories with you. Amara was diagnosed with Schizophrenia at age 28.

Introduction

Quick: Amara

Quick: Amara

Quick: Amara

Quick: Amara

Me: Yes, Quick

Quick: How do you spell schizophrenia?

Me: You've asked me this three times already. S, got it?

Quick: Yeah

Me: C, got it?

Quick: Yeah

Me: H, got it?

Quick: Yeah

Me: Oh, I can't remember anymore.

Quick: How are we going to write a book about

schizophrenia if you can't spell schizophrenia?

Me: Somehow, we'll do it Quick

You guys: What is the rest of the book about?

schizophrenia? That's boring.

Me: It's about alcoholism and schizophrenia, you guys,

o.k.?

You guys: Yeah, that's ok with us. We've got a lot to say

about that.

Musings of a Schizophrenic Drunk

Me: I'll put some of it in, but I must edit for the readers.

Quick: Hey Amara

Me: Yeah, Quick?

Quick: When did this all start?

Me: I think I'll start the story with the Beef Jerky sessions. That will be years after my first schizophrenic episode and years before my second. We'll talk about the alcoholism that shattered my fragile brain, the hospitals that crushed my strength and balance I acquired in the trees, and the painful recovery that left me dry and sober and sane. How's that sound Quick?

Quick: That sounds good, Amara

Conversations like this one go on in my head all the time, from time to time. The recovery is well under way, but the auditory hallucinations linger. I believe that one day they will stop and I will be left with peaceful silence to ponder what I can do next and right now. For today, I have "Quick" and "you guys" to comment on my comings and goings. I don't fight them because they will win. Instead, I solicited their assistance in drafting this memoir of mine, Musings of a Schizophrenic Drunk.

The words in *italicized* font were written in a delusional state. Some writings are from the hospitals, others I composed at home in different stages of the psychotic episode which took place over a period of months. The conversations between Quick, You guys, and Me take place inside my head and are commonly referred to as auditory hallucinations. The reflections at the end of some sections are my own.

Chapter 1
Beef Jerky

Sitting at the bar, on the patio, we began to talk about beef jerky. Jimmy Tee's recipe is the inspiration. Yeah, it's Jimmy Tee who brings it up, but I'm glad he does. I just love beef jerky. Turns out he knows how to make the best batch ever. I'm intrigued. All he needs is a kitchen and an oven; and I have those things.

Begin: Beef Jerky

Cowboy hat covers a greasy mat of gray hair. Plaid snap shirt reaches out to untrimmed fingernails and down to old jeans. Scuffed boots with pointed toes are well known in the two bars of Laporte, Colorado for the dancing they do. Jimmy Tee would stand out and be remembered just for his appearance, but he takes it one step further and begins to talk.

When Jimmy Tee spins his yarns to sitter-byers in the bar they are transported in time and space to days and places where they can feel good, free, and adventurous. An empty stool by Jimmy Tee is always filled before

Jimmy can buy his next drink. "Tell me a story, old timer; I'll get the next round." Jimmy got used to people saying that.

We have plenty of time to talk during our all night beef jerky dehydration sessions. As we share a 30 pack of Bud Light cans and check on the meat periodically, he tells me story after story from his colorful life. He fell from a 120 foot tree, caught a 5 pound trout in a frozen mountain stream, sang with Hank Williams, and had a million dollars in the bank. Or was the fish 120 pounds, and was it 5 dollars in the bank. It didn't matter with Jimmy Tee; the fun was in how he told the story.

Only his closest friends were witness to the beef jerky sessions. And, since it was my kitchen and I was willing to stay up with him all night to ensure a quality product (and that the beer didn't go bad) I was given a copy of the recipe. Jimmy Tee's Secret Sauce.

I think the reason he only let a select few in to the inner jerky circle was simple: when word got out that he licked his fingers between retrieving beef from marinade and cleaning the sauce from the meat before placing it in the dehydrator, sales went down considerably. It only took one brief visit from a distant friend for word to get out. Soon, the folks at the bar who were once willing to shell out five bucks for a bag of jerky had empty pockets when Jimmy Tee came around with his jerky.

Jimmy crashed on the floor of the 15 by 15 foot trailer box that Phil, the man this book is dedicated to, was renting after his run in with the law enforcement folks of Fort Collins. Phil encouraged Jimmy's endeavors: beef jerky and drinking, and also tried to influence Jimmy to shower from time to time. Phil stopped eating the Jerky when he woke up in the middle of the night and, from a cracked eyelid on the couch, he saw Jimmy separating the jerky into piles on the floor of the trailer kitchen. Phil couldn't recall the last time he cleaned the 2 by 3 foot space, and there and then, he decided to get his protein from another source.

On our first sales trip to pedal the jerky, Phil, happily drunk in the back seat of my car described our crew as a hippie, a red-neck, and a cowboy. With this combination, we were pretty sure there was no one we couldn't sell beef jerky to in Fort Collins. The business class was the only market we didn't feel we had an inlet to, but, really, the business class doesn't eat that much jerky anyway.

The three of us got into the habit of drinking heavily together. We'd pass bottles of cheap wine around the fire and empty case after case of cheap American beer.

One night I sat drunkenly blissed out on one of Phil's trailers between the red-neck and the cowboy. Jimmy was talking about something and soon Phil and I realized that we could no longer hear him. We had discovered that we both spoke Spanglish and were engaged in a conversation that probably meant nothing in any language. But, we kept talking, mixing English words with Spanish words and just having fun.

At some point, Phil reached over and put his hand on my neck and began to stroke my hair. It was the most erotic thing this hippie girl has ever felt. I knew I loved this redneck and wanted to know how I'd ever let him go. Getting up from the trailer was impossible; I hoped our cheap bottle of red wine would never be empty.

Of course the bottle did run dry and the three of us decided to drive drunkenly to the box that Phil called home. Phil and I shared a couch and Jimmy sort of slept on the floor next to us. We managed to keep our kissing quiet that night and I even slept for a few moments.

The big question the next day was if the beef jerky business could survive this new social development. And, when I called Jimmy later that day to schedule a meat pick up at the local butcher shop, he was displeased with my non-professional conduct on the couch. "You can't have my meat 'cause you slept on the couch with my friend last night." Which is something a drunk like Jimmy Tee might say. And, he did say that.

Jimmy recovered and learned to appreciate Phil's and my connection. We did go get more thinly sliced sirloin that afternoon. And, we all continued to share each others' company.

What can I say about Jimmy Tee? I read him a passage from this memoir and he asked to be included. So, Jimmy is an alcoholic who lives in his car so he can afford the drinks that keep him in the wrong company. Last night he got knocked on his ass because the door flew open from the push of a big, drunk man. He talked with the big man and the big man apologized. But,

Jimmy had to sit in his car today to let the hurt wear off.

Not emotional pain: it was an accident.

But, damn, when you're 68 and the door flies open on

your head: it hurts.

Chapter 2
Falling for Phil

Days went by, and I had time to think.   I decided what I want in a man and set out to see if Phil was the man for me. There are three things: (1) Respectful (2) Responsible (3) Really hot.

It's simple really. It is the three R's. Not reading, 'riting, 'rithmetic like they promised you, but: respectful, responsible, and really hot.

Phil's a jailbird now. I met him on his last days of freedom and his first days of sobriety. We kinda hit it off. Something like that.

Is he respectful and responsible? After a few nights together I'd say he was really hot. Yes, he is one out of three R's. Create an image in your head and it will arrive.

Responsible?
Respectful?
I'm hopeful.

They are all warning me about the jailbird. They say you can do better. But, the problem is I like him. I went to visit him in jail today. We sat together and talked about where we like to go in our heads when we feel blue.

It was really great. So, I'm continuing to like the guy against all the reasoning people are trying to do.

You can't win if you don't play.

Or, like Phil and I were saying today, we'll never know if we don't wait and see.

I'm not going to rush things and end it today. It will end itself of its own accord. All in its own time. Or, maybe it will last.

Yep, I'm in love with Phil. He is a landscaper with a big truck. He consumes much more fossil fuel than I should be ok with, if I was a self respecting hippie. I guess I'm not.

Musings of a Schizophrenic Drunk

The major challenge to falling in love this time is not forgetting that the rest of the world does exist out there. I have responsibilities you know.

If being around this guy kinda' makes me forget the rest of the world exists, is that good or bad? I'm gonna' say that it is good. Yes, very good.

I never want to go back out into it again. I just want to stay here in Phil's arms. But, when I do have to go out into it, it sure helps that he kisses me good luck as I go.

Time went by and Phil did his. Happily I invited him to move in with me when they kicked him out of jail. We got into sort of a routine of life while we got to know each other better. Our routine involved a lot of drinking.

Sometimes I get upset that Phil will leave me. And, other times he gets upset that I will leave him. I guess we both see how very different we are from each other. We even brush our teeth differently. I stand upright and keep the toothpaste mostly in my mouth. Phil hunches over the sink as spit and toothpaste run down his brush and coat his hand. He uses cold water and I use warm.

I try to talk to him about my schizophrenic demons and he shakes his head, "Honey, I don't have any idea what you are talking about."

He tries to tell me about his PTSD and I can't even imagine that any of it is real. He tells me it is real; I believe him. But, I can not feel it.

He talks engines.

I talk about brain structures and their functions.

I think our biggest fear is that we do actually have some things in common. And, I think, we do. Three things: alcoholism, drug addiction and mental illness. If you could choose the worst possible enabling traits, we share those too.

So, sometimes I wonder is this set of three problems is a solid basis for a long term relationship? What if one of us miraculously heals ourself? How will we relate?

Musings of a Schizophrenic Drunk

There is really nothing to worry about because from what I've seen neither of us has a chance. A stable mood and consistent outlook is something we'll never know.

And, really, I can read a book about brains while he beats his knuckles on greasy engines, but when I'm crying because I can't feel anything he knows that he can't help. I know I can't help him too when his demons cloud his vision with fear and hate.

So, our very different afflictions and demons will attack us both. So, we will love each other through those struggles even if we don't understand them.

We have only one thing in common: love.

When I met Phil, I was alone. I'd been recovering from schizophrenia for about four years and was still awkward with the world. I drank and did drugs to be around people. When I thought to myself, my writing looked like this:

"Do you have the right friends? Is your taste sophisticated? Are your drugs the right drugs? I don't. It's not. No.

But life goes on and I find joy in my own rhythm. I struggle with loneliness and voices in my head that tell me I'm not good enough. Today they echoed as I walked through seas of people: "why can you hear me today? Why aren't you out there?"

There is nobody out there but the wrong friends and drugs. So, sometimes I retreat to the voices inside my head. They aren't always nice, but they are always there.

So, there is always one more hit, one more glass of wine and the dawn always comes.

And, I stay in here. I am always joyful because I can go on to meet that dawn. And, I know that some days it is easy."

Musings of a Schizophrenic Drunk

Quick: Amara

Me: Yeah, Quick

Quick: What do you think?

Me: 'bout what Quick?

Quick: About the fact you've been hearing voices for so long now?

Me: I think it sucks Quick.

Quick: Ok, just wondering what you thought about it.

Chapter 3
Year One: A Party

Phil and I drank and partied with neighbors and friends, at the apartment we nicknamed "Davidson Dive", as we continued courting in our first year. I guess neither of us saw a reason to seek out sobriety. We were high on new love and both lost out of old relationships and ways of life. Drugs and alcohol induced jokes and good times, but we both could not manage the chemicals when we'd get too drunk or high, and we'd get angry and not know why.

See, I do have Schizophrenia, and when I get drunk long enough, it surfaces. It surfaces like an angry demon that wants to die. It lashes out at everything in its path with spit flying from its tongue. It seems to especially like attacking the ones I love.

It is me? It is my problem. That's all I know.

It's a deadly combination that I need to manage. It's happened a few times. I'd gone on six month drug and alcohol binges before, when I broke up with a serious boyfriend, or I was just embracing the freedom of being in my twenties and too dumb to realize forty was coming. More recently it just took two bowls of kind bud and 15-20 beers daily, and a few Valium over the period of a month to completely lose my feet on this Earth.

I've heard of bad drunks, and I even know a few. I'm much worse than that when I lose the drunk and get lost in meanness, confusion, and anger. It is a little difficult to explain this most recent (and last, I hope) event. It happened in a worsening progression. As it did the first time. But, this time I had one friend willing to tell me what happens when I get lost and can't remember.

The result is I need to not get drunk anymore.

The story is a sad one. I live with this friend, named Phil, and love him like no one I ever have. Four times this month, I fell asleep, blacked out, and woke up hearing voices I believed were coming from his mouth. I then began responding to the evil words, that I thought were coming from him, directed exactly directly at me. He was sleeping and I was crazed by voices in my head that I heard clearly coming from him.

My response involved all kinds of domestic violence. He managed to calm me every time. And, this last time, it was so bad; I did it in front of a group of people I didn't know. I woke alone not knowing what had happened still possessed by a shaking fear of what was coming next.

First, I went to walk alone to see if my head would clear.

I walked along a river until I found a cliff to scale. After I decided to not jump off the cliff, I returned to what I thought would be jail, hospital, or everything gone. I don't know why I didn't jump off that cliff. I think I figured that it wouldn't do the job, or I didn't want to die that way today.

Next, we talked; for some reason he talked to me again. I entered the unpleasant state of detox. After two and a half days of hurt, I lay in bed awake, fearing the nightmares of sleep. And, he slept in the lazy-boy across the room. I walked across the room to get a cigarette, and I remember, this time, what I heard. I heard something hurtful from his direction with his voice. I was two and half days into the detox and so I managed to not attack him or even confront him about it. I just decided to leave. He stopped me 'cause my presence outside the home would result in trouble for me. I wasn't looking, feeling, or thinking too well.

Four or five hours later he woke and I asked him why he said that. He said the conversation never happened. And, then I understood. I was hearing things due to the DT's. Which is quite similar to drug induced psychosis, and nobody's fault but my own. I need to monitor my alcohol intake.

It is hard to stop drinking when drinking is all that is around you. So, even pain like that doesn't stop me. Trouble follows.

I recover from my DT's or psychosis, whatever was happening, quickly. Weeks pass between episodes like this. Mostly we laugh, tell stories, and enjoy new love.

But alcohol always wins. Its aim is destruction. Not all was smooth.

Chapter 4
Getting Arrested

Not every alcoholic can be as lucky as I. I got thrown in jail with the man I love and it was sufficient reason for me to put the bottle down. Or, stop putting it down, however you want to look at it.

We'd been fucked up for about two days. Vodka, beer, and kind bud were staples around the apartment and a few days earlier resupply had arrived. I fell down and hit my head hard at least twice that night. Phil caught me a few other times. Eventually he had to gently hold me to the couch and hope I'd pass out so he could drink another beer in peace without fear of me splitting my head open and an unfortunate trip to the hospital putting a dent in the budget and most likely, landing someone in jail. When you're on felony probation with a domestic violence charge it doesn't go over well to pull into the emergency room drunk with a woman with her head split open. And, Phil was that felon.

He tells me I fell asleep and he was able to catch a few z's himself. The next day we woke still drunk and not ready for the 2 and a half hour drive we had scheduled to return a borrowed tractor. But, being the hard headed drunks we are, we checked to make sure, at least, the lights on the trailer worked before we headed out of Fort Collins and up the Poudre Valley to Steamboat Springs.

It was not a pleasant trip. I guess we've been living together for a time and my parents had lent him a tractor which we were returning; weather rain nor sleet nor snow. So, there was all of that. The weather was real bad. The roads were slick and the lanes were narrow.

We continued to argue. And the road wound on and on. Until, we came upon an unsuspecting liquor store, and purchased a pint of whiskey. In a few moments the empty, shattered glass hit the intersection cement.

We carried on, the tractor was delivered, the truck got stuck, we got away. Until, the big fight started. It is all in the police report if you care to wallow in the past. I'd leave that to the professionals. So, we were arrested.

I was arrested for assault. He had similar charges and was already in jail when I got there.

They gave me a nice cell. It had TV, TV dinners, a shower, hot water, cement, bars, and even gave me a pen to write my confession with. I was careful to put my confession in my pocket as I stepped up the steps to see the judge. Because I didn't know what confession he was looking for, I just answered his questions. So, the judge let me go, and asked me to report back to that same courtroom at a later date.

Unfortunately, things haven't gotten much better. Gonna' see a judge again in a few days. I'm sure I do not know what confession he is looking for so I hire an attorney. He has the story and is free from the emotions, so he will stick to matters at hand.

Phil and I drove to court together; the charges were dropped. We decided to give sober life a chance and see what it might hold for a couple of drunks like us. Phil was already required to be sober because he was on probation. So, we hopped on the wagon and held on tight.

Musings of a Schizophrenic Drunk

Three months on the government wagon: well, I've lost about ten pounds that I didn't even know I had to lose and now I can't buy a six pack, but I carry one around under my tee shirt.

We are precariously perched on Laporte Ave in Fort Collins Colorado. We live in the Bunker. The bunker is a 20 by 20 love shack that Phil and I have grown to call home. The owner recently remodeled it above and beyond the scope of any and all building permits. The walls are a foot thick, it has seven sets of lights, the floor is ceramic tile, the heater is nicknamed the dehydrator, and the windows open and close easily. The best feature of the bunker is the acre back yard where Phil stores his equipment and I have been stock piling shrubs and trees for the land we hope to purchase. The rent is the cheapest in Fort Collins at a low 475 a month with utilities included. I love it here, yet we are leaning forward into a strong gust of wind in order to stay balanced.

Strings pull us as we try to start a life together. My parents twist thumbs when acting on a offer co-sign a loan to help us purchase a raw piece of dirt where we hope to drill a well and water many plants. Phil's ex-wife sits on titles to his equipment as he struggles to pay her the divorce settlement from side jobs we do on the weekends. The government threatens to stop by for a house visit at any moment to search for weapons or alcohol because they say Phil went too far in a verbal argument he had over a year ago.

Jobs can be lost, titles signed over to banks, offers retracted, and we still be left with what few people go to bed with at night. Love. They can't take that, and if we hang in there and keep smilin' at the bosses and police officers we just might get out of here. The bunker is a great place to regroup and form a platform from which to build walls upon. After we get the walls built, I like to install a door and step out into the drive, start the car, let the engine warm up, and drive far away from these people who tried to build walls to keep me locked inside their rules.

I have to keep my story secret from people I meet. I can't tell them I was a drunken fool and got locked up for arguing with my boyfriend. I can't tell them I spent the night in a county jail waiting for someone to judge me and set a date to return. I can't tell them the reason I don't drink is because my lover is on felony probation and is required to check in with police officers each day to prove his sobriety. If I told them the story they would judge me and I would sacrifice strategic positioning in my battle to build my platform. They can't understand, and so they can't know, because it hasn't happened to them yet.

I'd like to tell them, "yes they put me in jail, but at least they had to handcuff me with five officers surrounding me. You are sitting in your own jail that you built yourself, with your programmed dreams, and manufactured ideals." But, maybe I just broke the law.

I spoke my mind and they arrested me. He spoke his mind and they arrested him. They called it domestic violence. Their solution was to put us in separate cells and try to keep us separated so we would turn deeper into an unresolved argument. We broke their rules (again) and talked back and forth between the cells. It took us about three words to make up, and once we were both out of the cells and safely violating the restraining order, it took a few moments to fall even deeper into love.

The Bunker year was wonderful. We both had jobs.
We'd go to work. We'd come home; eat dinner; and
listen to an AM short wave radio with a bent antenna.
Later, we'd make love. Sobriety pulled us tight together.

Quick: What happened then Amara?

Me: We remodeled a house Quick.

You guys: Quick, why are you asking Amara questions?
She is trying to write a book.

Quick: Oh, I don't know, I just want to know what
happened.

Me: I'm getting to that Quick.

Quick: Are you going to talk about the house now
Amara?

Me: Not so much. It's not a book about remodeling
houses. It's about alcoholism and Schizophrenia.

Quick: What about me?

Me: What about you, Quick?

Quick: I want the book to be about me.

Me: Well, you are a voice in my head. The
Schizophrenia part is about you.

Quick: When do I get to be in the book more?

Me: When I get sick Quick

Quick: I don't want you to be sick anymore Amara

Musings of a Schizophrenic Drunk

Me: Me neither, it would help if you and those guys
stopped talking to me so much

Quick: Ok Amara, keep writing

Chapter 5
The House and beyond

While we lived at the Bunker, we quit our jobs and got financing from my parents to remodel a 1910 house in old town Fort Collins. Eight months, seven days a week were filled with nails, sheet rock screws, wires, plumbing, exterior trim and paint, windows, sinks, toilets, texture, and tiles. We stayed sober and determined to flip a house to get out from under bills and move forward into a life we hoped to create.

Phil taught me to climb trees. We got licensed with the city to prune and remove trees of all sizes and shapes. We purchased equipment and started a tree company as the house project approached completion.

The economy dictated the times and the house didn't sell so we moved in and began to live there. Our money situation got worse and hopes of capital in the bank turned to empty pockets. We needed jobs again. Phil's probationary period with the law was nearing an end and things might have gone differently if we'd thought of a different way out of our money pit. But, instead we chose to spend a year on poor man's vacation: drinking away reality with the cash we could put in our pocket from small jobs around town.

Quick: What are you doing Amara?
You guys: She is writing a book Quick
Quick: Why is she doing that you guys?

Now, I sit in one of the front rooms of the house we remodeled scratching out this story of mine. The voices impede me more than help and I cling to my sobriety in fear of losing my stance in reality. Phil works forty hours in four days every week and we prune and remove trees together Friday through Sunday.

I've been out of the state hospital for a few months now and my strength and balance is beginning to return. I have shed five of the twenty five pounds I gained on my anti-psychotic medication diet. Each weekend, I am a little more of an arborist again; the limbs get lighter, the structure of the trees is more visible to me, and I can stay focused better to communicate with Phil, customers, and our ground guy.

As I am surrounded by activity and thoughtful people, the voices fade into silence.

Remembering the events that led up to my psychotic break is a trip through embarrassment and regret. Mistakes filled our time, after we completed the house we live in now, until the drunkenness, and arguments from drunkenness, finally allowed my illness to slip back in.

Chapter 6

Drunken Mistakes

I drank too much again

Again ?

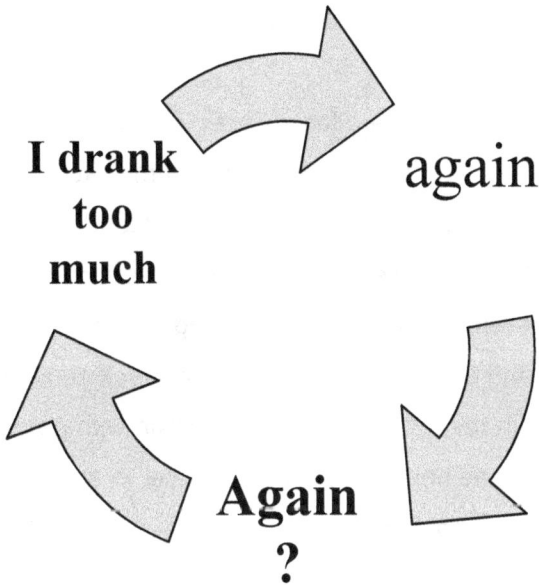

Well, it looks like good old Dad was right. Drinking did, in fact, ruin my life. I have fallen in love, worked hard for a future I felt I could function within, gotten extremely drunk, and it is all rapidly being stripped away.

If we hadn't gotten enough warnings, and I guess we hadn't, we screwed up one more time.

Deciding to visit the not so local pub in an unlicensed, uninsured vehicle, seemed like a good idea at the time. But when I had passed the point of blackoutness, and we were a few blocks from our home, I decided to exit the vehicle in a non-traditional manner. Yep, I just jumped out.

This created a problem for my brain. The main problem for my brain was that it was housed in my skull. And, my skull was not strong enough to withstand the slow reflexes that my lower limbs had after the alcohol. I could not remain upright, after exiting the mobile vehicle, and the impact landed on my weak skull, which fractured in response. This left my brain with a pool of blood that has been shifting, ever since, in an effort to exit the subdural layer.

Maybe, just maybe, the driver wouldn't have gotten that DUI if the witnesses hadn't noticed me moaning on the ground. And, probably not, 'cause we were almost home. Almost home in more ways than one: months from workin' off that deferred felony sentence, blocks from home and a warm bed, and work was soon to come in. Yet, when the blackout hit and the argument ensued, I jumped.

Musings of a Schizophrenic Drunk

So, here I am today facing all that I thought would be gone tomorrow and a few more charges. And, it makes my head hurt a lot more than it would have yesterday, because of that darn old blood on the brain.

My father said that I should not drink even one beer. He said it in a manner that made me feel he meant it. It really pissed me off.

Then, weeks later, there I was hurling myself onto surfaces that were moving much slower than I was. The result: pain and suffering. Perhaps, if I stop getting up: a ruined life.

After beating myself up thoroughly, I decided to survive. If I had made some bad decisions lately, and if they had cost me physical, judicial, and financial problems, it is not time to quit. If I have only one more day before my next drunken ill-doing (or, could it happen this way, sober mistake), I will not lie down and die without the hope that I can do it.

A remorseful drunk carries on....

Phil and I carried on together after this episode. He got a DUI and was sentenced to thirty days in County jail, his probationary period with the law was extended another two years, and his deferred sentence was deferred. He was now an official felon. I had months of recovery before any sort of movement wouldn't cause extreme pain.

We kept drinking. And, more mistakes were made. Phil changes on alcohol; Amara changes on alcohol. Our fights made no sense in reality; but drunk, exhausted, and angry was a place we chose to visit together many times.

My blackouts brought on psychosis.

I have been known to lose my mind, from time to time. Usually, due to wine.

It happens, sometimes when I don't expect it. It also happens, when I can see it comin' at me for miles and I can't look away from the headlights. I've tried to drink in almost every manner possible and each new method leaves something to be desired.

Please don't call me a quitter. I've given it all I have.

I'm writing this message to you one peck at a time with my left hand, because it seems my last binge has rendered my right hand fairly useless for quite some time to come. I can get the stitches out in two weeks, and hopefully (upon editing: it has been well past a year and internal damage remains) the internal shock will heal within the month.

I work and play with my hands. For now, I have time to reflect on the madness that enters my mind when the alcohol saturates it. This is not a reflection of myself that I like to visit. Actually, it scares me, it saddens me, and it won't go away.

I have to clean and put ointment on the wounds, that are bound by sixty stitches, twice a day at least. I have never been more repulsed by my body than I am now when I tend to my right hand and forearm.(Something to remember). See, I was drunk and angry, and I let the madness in my mind.

I lost control of my controls.

After reflecting on the conversation with the paramedic, during the ambulance ride, I have new thoughts about anger and blood pressure.

They took my blood pressure and the reading came back a beautiful 120 over 80. I said, "That's pretty good." The paramedic agreed and added that he felt it especially good for someone who just punched her hand through four separate windows.

Now, that I have so much time to think, and attempt to decode the blackout that involved this window smashing rampage, I wonder if my blood pressure was getting too high as I argued. And, blood letting seemed the fastest solution to the elevated blood pressure level problem.

Perhaps I am giving drunken Amara too much credit. Could I have really been monitoring my body that closely? That's a stretch. I guess I just punched the window 'cause I was mad.

Well, anyway, still sittin' here sober thinkin' about it.

Musings of a Schizophrenic Drunk

Recovering from bad drunks took up a lot of time that year. But, we weren't done yet; we were down low, but the bottom hadn't fallen out. Phil still had to go to jail and I hadn't been arrested yet or to the hospital with full blown psychosis. So, we'd try to keep drinking.

Time to address the drunken issue. I am drunk too much of the time. A low grade buzz is an acceptable mode to pass through most all of life, but drunken spells need to be numbered. Well, mine are numbered right now, but it is a large number.

I have blacked out probably 5 times in the past two weeks. Now, I'm an alcoholic, so a blackout is a pretty easy place for me to find. That does not mean that I like that place. I prefer to remember my life.

That's why we got a handy dandy breathalyzer. I can self administer a breathalyzer test at any time. Tonight I kept myself from having a blackout by these self tests. At 6:10 I was a 0.12 and felt just fine. 0.08 is the legal limit for a DUI in Colorado and you can get a DWI with a 0.04. So, at 0.12 I was working on a good buzz. And, from the experimentation I've been doing with the breathalyzer it seems that I am approaching blackout conditions at 2.5. So, when I reached 0.12 I stopped drinking. Yep, mid Bud Light I stopped. And now, at 7PM I am a 0.08. I can not drive tonight, but I am moving away from blackout territory.

So, now I can remember how nice it is when Phil comes walking in that door. I admit that I am still not certain he is coming back at the end of the day. Self doubt twists in my gut each day as I wait for his return. Did I scare him away last night in my blackout??

Sounds possible, doesn't it? Scaring someone away in a blackout is something I could very easily do. Yet, I've been blacked out with him for the past 5 blackouts and he is still here.

This doesn't make me think that blackouts are ok or that I must be a real charmer in that alternate state. Rather, it makes me want to stop having blackouts!!!!!!!!!!!!!!!

We joke sarcastically about everything except being drunk.

Quick: Kinda' immature, Amara

Musings of a Schizophrenic Drunk

Me: What Quick?

Quick: You guys are being kinda' immature, in the book, right now.

Me: Really, Quick, do you have a comment for the book?

Quick: Yeah, I do, Amara.

Me: Go ahead.

Quick: That's it. You guys are acting immature. Drinking and being sarcastic and stuff.

Phil and I had both experimented with the AA program. And, since things were getting so bad, we decided to write up a few of our own steps that we hoped would help us stay out of trouble.

Step One

Do not build propane fires inside. Ever.
Never introduce fire into a enclosed area without proper supervision!!!! A semi- sober person in the area.

Step Two

DO NOT deny thy friend beer when there be only two left.

Step Three

Thou should always have water on hand.

IMPORTANT NOTE: consume water at equal rate to alcohol at all times.

Step Four

(This is an important step, read it twice.)

Thou shalt never have guns in thy presence when shitfaced

Step Five

This step is for couples. Evaluate your BAC (blood alcohol content) when you discuss issues. You can keep a chart or you can make mental notes.

This is what you are keeping track of:

How you feel when you discuss a topic and what your BAC is when you are engaged. Adjust your conversations so you discuss the topics that give you the best emotional state. You can decide what emotional state you want to arrive at, but the one that people seem to like best doesn't put them in jail. To reiterate, BAC level, topic choice, and emotional state.

Step Five is as far as we got. Looking back, we probably should not have tried to do things our way.

Chapter 7
'A Delayed Recovery' or 'Now I get really sick'

I almost lost my life. Again. I spent more than a year struggling to build a life with the man I love the most. The past few months, we have spent wallowing in self pity and drunkenness wishing things would go our way. Now, that the jobs have started to trickle in, we can't seem to feel good about anything.

Our arguments go in circles and always back to walls we can't climb. I don't even know what we're angry about anymore. We just don't seem to want to be around each other. So, he's mad, and then I'm mad. Never at the same time, and then we draw each other into it. He blames me, and then I blame him. Then we both blame ourselves alone.

Nothing we said we'd do is happening. One day we promise to go to church together. Then, Sunday rolls around, and we get drunk before the service begins. We talk about going fishing, then the sun comes up, and beer is cheaper than a fishing license and gas money to get to the river.

Musings of a Schizophrenic Drunk

I got drunk and belligerent, because I feel my life slipping away. I considered taking my life and giving it to the devil. I had promised Phil the day before that I would never try to die again, and so I called the hospital on myself and asked them if they could calm me down; with drugs or talk, it didn't matter to me. They came quickly with lights flashing and rushed me to situation worse than the one I'd come from. They didn't want to calm me, they wanted to start a new argument with me. So, I became more belligerent and ended up in another mental ward.

I managed to convince the teams of doctors, staff people, and other patients that I was just a wicked alcoholic and not crazy. But, it was a close one. They tried to medicate me and send me to place where I'd never truly feel calm again. I don't know what I needed.

I read the bible as much as I was allowed to in the ward. And, I prayed for God to clear my mind and put the right words into my voice. They let me out and I returned to the original argument.

I need to make friends and get a life. These are things I was trying to do when I was single and I met Phil. So, now I'm single again, but in a relationship? I would like to make a life with Phil, make friends with Phil, walk and hike and fish with Phil. But, he says he doesn't walk, he doesn't want to stop drinking, and that he is only awaiting homelessness. So, I must make a new life for myself. Because if my only option here is to drink, and I can't drink, and I can't be around people who drink, I need to find new people to be around. I will start making new friends, and if my friends and Phil's friends are different friends, I don't see that as a life I want.

As far as him drinking less and spending time with me doing things while we're not drinking that's an option he won't consider. He'd rather end our relationship and continue to love the bottle and people who will wallow in it with him.

I came back from the hospital in a strange mood. And, I needed to talk. He wanted to have fun with his friend and suggested that I clean the house. I felt trapped in the house like I felt trapped in the hospital. I can't get angry and drunk because I am frustrated with a man who won't walk or hike with me. I will lose my life, because if I continue to drink and be angry, I will die or someone will rescue me and put me back in the hospital.

I want a healthy life with the man I love. I want to wake up drink coffee, work, walk, hike, fish, listen to music, make music, make love, laugh, and live. I can't beg anymore for him to love us. He has concerns that he sees outweigh any chance of us being happy. I am unsure of what I should do.

I am scared of him, and he is scared of me.

We can't talk anymore. I can't ask for help anymore when it just makes him mad. I can't help anymore because I have nothing left to give.

I pray for God to help us stay together and be healthy. I do not know what he prays for. I wish I knew how to help us love again.

You guys: Sounds like you are pretty bad drunks, Amara
Me: Yeah, we were and it brought my Schizophrenia back, that's you guys

Amara Lorch

You guys: We're back, but.....
Me: But what?

I think we are falling out of love. It has been a subtle thing, but it happened. More and more we fall asleep in different locations. He seems to resent my hard times and I tend to care less and less about his. We are falling out of love.

Things are too hard now; we are too drunk too much of the time now. Phil is slowly moving out and we are both being crushed with the sadness of losing love and friendship. I can't think anymore; it seems that neither can he. I begin to experience psychosis and do not tell anybody because I do not know what is happening. The friendship and good feelings that usually fill our time between drunken mistakes fades to zero, as my mind does not snap back after drinking anymore, and I get lost inside my head. I draw away from Phil's attempts at resolution: he suggests a hike in the canyon or a walk by the river. I refuse, and communicate only with my delusions. My mind is sick now. I insist Phil moves out of our house.

Musings of a Schizophrenic Drunk

I can still follow schedules and make appointments as the schizophrenia settles in my brain. Tomorrow we are scheduled to go to work. So, we will work.

Schizophrenia comes on strangely. Stress of arguments, our relationship falling apart, trying to make a living, and fighting addiction broke my connection with reality. I began to believe everyone was watching me and yet I was able to put on the appearance of a functioning human being. We went to work this day and I communicated about the tasks at hand. But, I was sure the line of school buses that drove by, when I was in the treetop, was filled with hateful sentiment and wanted me to die.

An angry parade passed by this morning. A stream of children, who had no idea why they were being paraded around instead of running free or hitting the mathematics and grammar books, were in this parade. I don't think some people wanted me to enjoy my passion and talent. I almost lost the focus that I gained as I slowly stepped up a long rope to get to my work.

But, the tree waited for me to clear my head and I checked my belt to see what I had brought with me to move around the tree. This tree is a burnt out Elm whose branches fall, unexpectedly, when children, old folks, people in wheelchairs, people in cars, healthy people, parked cars, and people on bikes move unsuspectingly across the parking lot in front of the trailers and in back of the laundrymat. I was hired to be part of the tree service that will remove this hazard from Earth.

The wood is hardwood and will make fine firewood next season. The chip will be a hassle to discard. The fun stuff happens in the tree. In the tree, I have an orange lanyard, some carabineers, water, a rescue knife, webbing, a handsaw, a chainsaw, and my climbing line is hooked to a swivel. I get to take fun rides, after a cut, when the weight comes off the limbs that are left. I get to hold angry saws in my hands and let them do the work. I have stiff boots that keep my feet from cramping and protect my toes. My helmet is blue and has my title on it: Bad Bunny.

A little less than one fourth of the tree came down today, without incident. Not even a close call worth telling around a campfire or in these musings. Maybe all the folks who hope for train wrecks will get lucky tomorrow and a nice sharp split will pierce my face and exit through the back of my helmet. Or, a saw could act like chainsaws sometimes do and jump right through my leg, allowing the blood in my body to flow freely to the ground and form a puddle. Then, someone else will have to do the job.

That would be inconvenient for the people who need to pass through that parking lot from time to time. And, the animals too.

I was so angry at imaginary opinions that day. I broke up with Phil because I also believed he wanted to see me fail. In reality, it was an awesome day of work.

Delusions occupied my brain, all day and night, telling me Phil was cheating on me, the kids in the buses wanted me to die, and the film crews were watching me climb and work. From my position in the tree where I was removing limbs, I spotted the van that had the film crew in it and wondered what kind of microphones they were using that could hear what I was saying from so far away. There was not a film crew in the neighborhood. My thoughts felt read and exposed to the world and I was sure the people I was watching on TV the night before were with me in the tree tracking my progress.

Delusions slowed me and I took steps in mud.

Sometimes life slows down so slow I think that I am dying. Like now. I have made a few decisions lately. I am becoming a sober bunny, breaking up with a man with whom a relationship is not working, and determined to notice beautiful things. But, everything is real slow. We are still breaking up, but the jobs that would provide the money to get us out of the same house are not arriving. Sometimes I cannot see beauty because I am run down by the way the walls are caving in as I try to climb back to ground level.

I don't think I'll die today, and if I manage to stay busy, maybe I won't feel like I'm dying. That would be good.

So, I have already entered a delusional state, I am forcing a breakup with Phil, and I think everything is ok and that I am rebuilding a life which will include all my new delusional friends, one of which is going to marry me and have kids with me and we will have lots of fun always. All the problems of my real life relationship would be solved by my delusion man: he promised he didn't drink and he promised, in my hallucinations, that he was perfect for me.

Phil was still there, we were doing what we love (working in the trees), and he was ready to try again. For me though it was too late - sickness occupied my brain. When he tries to talk to me about us and what is happening I am too upset and confused in delusions to be there. I am starting to believe he has been cheating on me, he has locked me in a box with snakes for days, he never really loved me, and I can't communicate or explain any of it. It is some real relationship stuff mixed hopelessly in with hallucinations and delusions. I push him away and the delusions become stronger.

I don't know why God does what he does. I believe that everything that happens on Earth is according to God's plan. That is what I believe.

It feels like things are going to be a lot better in my life now that my relationship with Phil is over. It also feels like things are going to be extremely difficult at times. I am willing to do the best I can in order to remain free of Phil.

I have made the same mistakes over and over again in my life. I will remember what he did so that I do not believe lies dressed in sheep's clothing. When I went to his trailer to return his truck, he was vacuuming. He taught me to ash my cigarette on the floor of what was supposed to be our house. He took the caulk that we bought to seal the airflow around a window in the house that was supposed to be ours, to seal the air flow around a window in his new trailer. The caulk had been here available for use in our house long before he was kicked out. He is concerned about his heating bill. Funny, he didn't seem to care about our heating bill. The list goes on and on.

If outsiders could see what was going on, no one ever mentioned it to me. I couldn't see it. I read in a study about relationships ending that the loss you feel over losing future dreams and plans is more painful than practical. That meant to me that in bad relationships, when you keep hitting your head against a wall and trying to make it work so you can get all those future dreams you have made up, it is not a practical loss you are feeling because those things would really never happen. I thought he loved me and I believed the lies he told to me and the ones he told to himself. I want to scream out to world, "Why didn't you tell me?" When I can manage to not be angry it is because I believe that people in general, not just me, have to learn the hard way. I didn't think it would be this hard because I didn't know how bad it was and all the things that had happened. (Locking me up with snakes is bad.) No one could have explained it to me in a way I would understand until I was ready. I want to scream out at myself, but what could I scream, I never listen anyway.

So, I got myself into a lot worse trouble than I was in before, by not paying attention.

I'm happy today because Phil moved out of our house. I feel less sick in mind and body than I have for a long time. I feel like I have an opportunity to live again and that I can make it through this life. For the last couple of years, I told Phil many times that we could do it and blah, blah, blah. I felt sicker and sicker everyday I kept trying to make our relationship work in the midst of our abusive relationship with substances.

I cried today in the kitchen because the arresting officer I dream about treats me like a lady. I am still shattered Amara. I will be strong and beautiful the day we meet. Right now I am weak and frightened. I will not be angry when we meet. Right now, I have red hot bolts of anger shooting through my body at random times for random reasons.

The red hot bolts of anger are physical symptoms of schizophrenia. They are uncomfortable and scary. I am home alone; Phil lives down the street. I write out delusional thoughts about how the delusional man will meet me later and I am incapable of speaking to Phil about our problems. I can only write to myself.

You guys: Who's the cop, Amara?
Me: That's a delusion you guys. I was arrested a few weeks before that tree job I was writing about and since then delusions and hallucinations have been courting me in the form of a cop, driving a wedge between me and Phil.
You guys: What are you talking about Amara?
Me: It's you guys before I knew you were voices in my head telling me to do things like kick Phil out of our house and marry you instead.

Musings of a Schizophrenic Drunk

You guys: We're sorry; we're not sorry; we're sorry; we're really not.
Me: Shut up.

At this point, I kick Phil out and think a cop is coming to whisk me away into romance when the time is right. I'm very sick and alone and no one understands why I am acting the way I am.

We continue to work together in the trees. I get more distant. Phil believes it is because of the break up; my writings show me it is due to delusions and growing sickness.

Even with all the adrenaline, satisfaction, and warm weather, if I wasn't getting so much help, now would be about the time I marshmallow up and get back together with Phil. I'd try to make everybody feel better, especially the ones who have hurt me the most. I'd end up black and crispy on the outside and a dripping, gooey mess on the inside. Then, somebody would chew me up and spit me out.

Thank you for the help. (This was directed at the cop who wants to marry me at a later date).

Amara Lorch

I feel that if the world could see me now, a lot of them would hate me. I'd need a real good security system to fend off death attempts. For what? I guess I shouldn't try to live my life the way that feels good to me. I am real sad, a moment ago, for all the bunnies like me who just don't know what to do most of the time. So many walls, shots, and hits when they try to shine, that giving up, seems like a good idea at the time.

Being hated doesn't feel too good. Giving up feels worse.

I had a good day of work today. I removed a bigger branch than I'd ever removed. If I didn't have brain damage (I believed I had serious brain damage and was about to die at any moment.), *it probably would have been real scary. Instead, I was clear and focused. The branch I was standing on didn't bounce too much; it was a solid lead from the giant trunk of an Elm tree. If my luck keeps up, I'll get to climb that tree again.*

I sure like it in the tree better than on the ground. When I got down, a man told me I was his wife. That's funny, I will marry the man who asked.

Musings of a Schizophrenic Drunk

If that was the question. I hope so.

Phil was the man who said I was his wife that day. He didn't understand why I was so set on breaking up. We were working as a team to do tree work only a match made in heaven could do. I thought the cop who proposed, over and over, in my head was my fiancé. I hurt and left Phil when I was sick with a debilitating disease that twisted my mind, put me in a fantasy world, and ruined my chance of healing with Phil.

We were both ready to stop drinking, but it was too late. I no longer understood what was real and what was not real.

Today, I still have voices pestering me. They are lingering aftereffects of my psychotic break. But, I only believe what I can see, feel, and hear on the outside of my body. I am still frightened of using my imagination at times. I am operating on empirical evidence only. I recover with lingering auditory hallucinations in my head. I definitely am not taking any advice from my voices.

Chapter 8
Alone in Sickness

I continue to live in our house alone slipping deeper into delusions after Phil moves down the street.

I can't sleep yet this night. But, I've been eating real good which I think counts for something. Kinda' feel like I have no idea what has happened for my whole life. Couldn't have been that bad 'cause I'm still here.

Everything is stranger and more up in the air than ever before. I feel like I've never been here before. Almost always, I feel like everybody knows more about what is going on than I do.

I guess I'll set up a few guidelines for myself to follow throughout this confusion. Wish I knew what would be the right ones and I wish, more, I knew what the wrong ones were. Sometimes I think my actions have led to a stable state; I wonder what I did then. Those must have been a great couple of days. I bet I was active, slept, and thought about things I could work towards achieving.

Musings of a Schizophrenic Drunk

I might be more in tune with the rhythm around me if I listened. Sometimes I'm a good listener; mostly I talk a lot to myself.

Whatever has caused me to walk the ways I did is long gone. I am just stumbling along trying to get a decent foothold. They are everywhere: I found a stub to rest my foot upon a few days ago in an Elm tree and I was actually able to step up and advance from there to get to the hanger I needed to prune from that tree; today I set my feet into soft melting sugar snow and leaned with full force into a green machine that had wheels but no self propulsion; when I step out my backdoor after a snowstorm and a warm day, I step over the ice sheet that forms; when I climb out of a swimming pool I get my foot solid on the ledge before I lift myself onto slippery tiles, and I fall down when I miss.

So, what is really going on that I can't even talk to myself about events and have to bury my thoughts in so deep? I'd like to start a new life 'cause this one is fucked.

I guess that could be a guideline: "Don't do things that make me feel fucked."

Walking around is alright, I'd like to keep trying to work at things I can do well, and learn a few new things before I die. Just 'gonna stop doing things that don't feel right to me.

This is especially important to me right now for a few reasons. (1) I have no idea what is going on really. (2) The things I've been doing lately that don't make me feel good make me feel real bad. (3) I have a long way to go on this planet; God has been more than generous with me and I'd like to be a more active participant in my own survival.

Right now I am not proud of how I live. I'd like to plea stupidity, but that really doesn't satisfy me. Why have I let my life spiral out of my control? When did reasoning become unreasonable and why didn't I notice? Sure, some was trust in weak branches that looked real good on the outside. And, a lot of it was pretending not to notice. I didn't want to notice when my plans left the timeline I thought I was on, and so kept waiting for the life to begin long after I thought it should have started.

Musings of a Schizophrenic Drunk

When I wrote this attempt at setting myself guidelines, I was sitting at home alone, writing to myself, wondering where everybody and everything went. I am operating without proper tools in my brain kit. And, I can't think my way out of this one.

I start cleaning the house, organizing drawers, and other small tasks that sort of make sense. Yet, I have no concept of the larger picture of life. I will have to make a living and rebuild a life. Those things seem non-existent to me. I am lost in delusions, and sickness has swept away my ability to function in the world. I live in my head.

At this same time, Phil is cleaning his new house and, since he is not lost in delusions, figuring a way out of the mess we left. When his world stops spinning he comes and looks for me. Even before, he stops by the house to check on me and see how I am. I am delusional. I yell at him for locking me in a box with snakes which he didn't do, and other sorts of schizophrenic delusions.

I felt pretty good today for awhile. It seems like when I go out there people are sometimes drawn to me, sometimes pushing away from me, sometimes not noticing I'm there at all, and sometimes trying to draw me into what's going on over there.

I was happy today when I was trying to get as close to the ducks as I could before they flew away. I could not get very close because the snow was crunchy, from the warm weather followed by the cold.

It took a few moments before I let what was not at the river disappear. It did for a few moments. My head was free and the good things that were not at the river flowed in and bubbled for a while.

I walked to a place I'd seen the ducks before. When I arrived, I thought they were not there. I knelt, watched the half frozen river flow by, and prayed. When I had thanked God for a few things, I noticed a Drake paddling around upstream. I was happy to see him because I like to watch the cold water roll off his feathers when he comes up from diving for bugs. I crept closer to get a better look, and he flew off. A Hen was hidden behind the riverbank; I could not see her until he took flight.

Musings of a Schizophrenic Drunk

They flew off together; it looked like they were heading upstream.

I was disappointed because I spooked them so I sat still. A ripple in the water led my sight to another pair of ducks just a little further away than the two that flew away. I crawled and walked along a wash that had no crunchy snow in it: to make less noise. At last, I had to step on a hard piece of snow to get closer; the two flew away. It looked like they were heading upstream too.

When I left, through the frozen snow, I thanked God especially for showing me where the ducks were. And, I thanked him for my troubles and the help.

The help, again, was not Phil climbing a tree with me like I needed. The help, this time, were the voices in my head telling me I was doing the right thing walking aimlessly around this planet watching ducks, thanking God, and not relating to people or real situations. I had no money, food was running short, and I no longer checked phones, newspapers, computers or people for information. I was being led about by the voices in my head.

I can't forget an unfortunate series of events that I can not remember. This blank memory is teaching me quite a bit about the grip I need to get on my problems. I am considering, from time to time, making a list of questions to ask a psychiatrist. I will divide the list into two categories: alcoholism and mental illness. The shrink I ask will be intelligent and insightful. I need feedback 'cause these echoes in my head offer a little less than solutions.

Echoes fall short, when I think about alcoholism. They come back at me in jokes and rhymes; I don't know if they take it seriously. Even with all the consequences, they still keep me laughing.

Echoes fall short, when I think about mental illness. They shrug and say, "That's a tough one." "It is a real head scratcher."

Quick: I'll be your therapist Amara.
Me: Quick?

Musings of a Schizophrenic Drunk

Quick: Yeah, it's me, let me try to help you.

Me: Alright. Doctor, I have these problems…

Quick: I'm not a doctor. I'm a clinician.

Me: Ok, clinician, I have these problems….

Quick: How so?

Me: I have been diagnosed with Alcoholism and Schizophrenia. What is your prognosis?

Quick: Well, Amara, those are both incurable.

You guys: Doesn't sound too good, doc.

Quick: I am not a doctor. I am a clinician. But, well, let me see here, Miss Amara, I think, well, ummm… ah yes, I know how to fix it.

Me: How?

Quick: See, you're incorrigible dear. I believe this will do your long term recovery some good.

Me: What does that mean?

Quick: Incorrigible?

Me: Yeah.

Quick: It means, depraved beyond reform, Amara.

Me: That's good?

Quick: In your case, yes. It may allow you a few laughs and less pain as you begin to understand the gravity of your situation as a Schizophrenic drunk.

Me: Quick?

Quick: Yeah, Amara?

Amara Lorch

Me: You're kinda' a pain in the ass.

There was no one to talk to.

*Always seems like it is a good time in my life when I find
a new name. I'm Woodsie The Bunny now. I live under
a big log beside a bend in the river. The log that covers
the entrance to my burrow was a snag; long dead
standing timber that fell down one day in a strong wind.
I like the way it worked out because there was soft dirt
around a root system right where the best branches for
predator defense landed. The dirt was easy to move as
I made my home around the roots that scaffold neat little
rooms. I can drop droppings, store hay, stretch out, and
when it is time to hop I have just the right branches
smashed down on top of the entrance that I can sniff for
foxes, eagles, and snakes before I go out. They haven't
got me yet. It has only been a few days since I became
Woodsie The Bunny. It feels good.*

*I like living in the woods much better than those days of
scampering through sticky, itchy weeds. All the
seasons have a lot to offer in the woods. Springtime*

brings juicy green sprigs of plants I've never seen before. Summer is hot sometimes; I will lap up fresh water from the river to cool. Fall is going to be like winning the lotto; so many leaves under my paws to graze upon and store in one of my nice new rooms that the roots scaffold; I might get fat. Winter will be a time to leave tracks all over the forest floor.

It is good to be Woodsie. 'Bout time.

A year is not such a long time for a bunny. I've never been Woodsie The Bunny before; I imagine I'll have so much to learn about rabbit activities that it will be next year before I know it. I'll have lots of stories to tell. They won't be all these old boring stories that run circles in my head and make me sad and angry. The new stories will be ones that are not in this book and I will share them with the man in my dreams. He tells me he is not a bunny. I think he is a duck. I'm looking forward to hearing what this duck thinks about and hopping along at his side.

You guys: Were you really a rabbit, Amara? Or did you think you were one?

Me: No, it just seemed nicer to pretend. And, wait for dream man. Or, should I call him delusion man. He tells me he will marry me in a year.

You guys: Delusion man is better.

You guys: That's funny isn't it guys?

You guys: Yeah, that's funny. We tricked her good.

Still, no one to talk to during the day. So, I write this account of Schizophrenia alone with auditory hallucinations hassling me. Thank God, Phil comes home at night and we talk about our tree work, dinner, politics, life, love and dreams. It turns out that this year of building new stories is happening as I hop along at Phil's side. Funny thing about delusions is that they are not real; they just kept me away from real things. Phil is real and he was here, in reality, waiting for me when I came back.

I am not sure what the job involves. I have put my application in to the higher ups. And, I believe they are considering what I might be capable of in their army. An army takes a lot of "who's its" and "what's its" to win.

Musings of a Schizophrenic Drunk

They are considering what Woodsie might do for the army of God.

I don't think I need to list my experiences and skills. I think they got it. I am ready to fight in and with the army of God. So, I keep sending my application out and about to various agencies. And, I will answer when the call comes down from the heavens and calls Woodsie, that's me, to win.

What will the camps be like? Do we get resupplied? Or, do we get fucked on supplies? Do we give up yet? Do we play chicken and try to get out of the next day's battle? Do we rest when rest is not possible? Yes, we do the impossible: everyday and the next day.

I'll be in the hospital soon; I don't know it is coming. I think I am in God's army. Each day gets stranger as I am left alone with my thoughts. And, sometimes I drink to fight off the voices. It doesn't work.

So, I'm considering putting the bottles up on the wall for the night. How am I going to do that? I will bend my elbows a little bit; I will wrap my fingers around the straps; and I will give a tug. This might pull my garter straps up enough to stop the harassment that drives me to drink with an insatiable appetite. I do doubt that. The harassment will never end. The opinions refuse to find hobbies. Extreme interest in my demise is the focus of a lot of the loud opinions in my head.

If the opinions ask me what about before, I'd say, "that's is why I'm here." It ain't been pretty for a while. Workin' on moving from one abuse to another; and if all goes well, the abuse may end. Not before they get their shot at thinking their abuse is the best kind of abuse. (They are voices in my head.)

So, I'm just sittin' here trying to get drunk enough to fend off nightmares for a while and the voices won't stop. And, that's ok. 'Cause I'm in love and I am trying to heal. This involves rest and work.

Like the original plan, I will stop drinking when the beers are gone. I'm pretty much there.

I'm not really doing anything at this point. Phil has moved out. He stops by to check on me from time to time. I get angry, due to the delusions, and run him off.

Musings of a Schizophrenic Drunk

I just circle about in my head: one day angry, one day happy, one day I'm a rabbit, the next day I'm not.

I do manage to remember that I am due at alternative sentencing as a result of my arrest a few months back. I go there, but I am not there.

Weekenders (an alternative jail sentence), probation, court dates, and alcohol class all required my attention and attendance. It is confusing for me.

I am beginning to hear a lot of voices in my head and believed they were the people around me talking to me. The night before my workender experience, I lay on the couch and watched the clock skip numbers. Sometimes they would roll along at an alarming rate. I thought the cops had control of the clock and were trying to make me late for the day of work. Really, this is what happens in a catatonic state of mind. I called Phil that night and yelled at him about delusional angers. He called me back and calmed me down thinking I was just angry and upset. I woke and did what I was required to do, tried to do things that didn't make me feel fucked, and fell deeper into psychosis.

My pack is filled with the required items and a few things they didn't think I might need. Water is an extra item I packed in my left side pocket; looking forward. Tampons are in the right side pocket; looking forward. I hope the paperwork I will provide will let me in the door. Now, I am going to let my sweet little truck warm up cause it's cold outside.

Half way to day one of weekenders I realized that in all the exhaustion, excitement, and joy of getting my own wheels the day before, the concept of registration and insurance had slipped past my mind. It seemed like a real bad idea at the time to drive and park at the jail in a vehicle of that status, but a no show would possibly bring worse consequences, a warrant? I didn't know what would be worse and I was half way there so I kept going.

My paperwork was insufficient, at best. I had to spend some time on the "hot" bench while they shuffled my missing papers away. Then, a tall brunette made me count into a machine until he said stop to see if I am drunk. I got an orange vest that was impossible to slip over my work wear without exposing my mid-drift. I'd never been to weekenders before, so I didn't know how to dress for the vest.

I got to talk to lots of people. More people than I've talked to in a long while. We talked about books, injuries, illnesses, played games, made jokes, laughed, listened to an informative talk (Which I'll probably hear again, if the doctor ok's me to work, in the condition I am in.), and I filled out a form. The form almost made me cry; I went to the bathroom and splashed water on my face. Forms and I are not like PB and J.

When I came out of the bathroom, the room was silent. I locked eyes with a gentleman jail bunny, his presence made my survival instincts kick in, and I got real serious for some reason. I'm glad he was so far away; I was already in enough trouble without finding out who he was and why he made me relax in such a strange way. It felt like when I'm ready to lay that angry chain down on a limb that serves no useful purpose to a tree that is under my care.

That is when I scooted down the bench and some girl jail bunnies and I found a board game and played a little bit of the game of Life. Nobody won, of course.

Then, they kicked me out and I was told that I got no credit. I'm not sure what they meant. But, thinking about it now, no credit is better than bad credit.

I drove home, directly home. I did not pass go; I did not pay 200 dollars. Jail is there for me though. It is right down the street on Prospect and Timberline. I know a good way to get there on my bike; if I am in a hurry, I know a few routes to drive my truck.

It's not really fun to think about the 160 hours of labor that I am sentenced to coming up for me. So, I write about events in my life like this, to help the time pass.

Chapter 9
My Trip to the Hospital

Things got stranger and stranger in my lonely world before they finally came and drove my away in an ambulance. For a while, I was convinced by my delusions I was dying. I felt so psychically sick that it was easy to believe. I was scared, alone and dying. I didn't know what to do, and I wanted to smoke another cigarette before I died. I walked down the block to the 7-11 and bought a pack of smokes. I felt like I was floating as I walked through the dark night. People talked telepathically to me on the street, telling me how awful I looked and that I was probably dying.

When I got back to the house, I was locked out. My delusions were forcing me to believe terrible, untrue things, that had no basis in reality, about Phil and how he never loved me and terrible affairs he had had. If a person is not sick with Schizophrenia, they can hear a lie or wild story and be mildly affected by it or not at all. Schizophrenia or psychosis, in general, gives the term "believing" a whole new meaning. When I was sick with psychosis, believing felt painful everywhere in my mind and body.

I struggled with a window as I tried to enter the house. Then, I collapsed on the back patio and began to dry heave the meals I hadn't been eating the past few days. I saw and heard demonic voices and shapes all around and in me, as my stomach convulsed. I thought I was going to hell.

I passed out.

I came to and I was still scared. In the scramble of auditory and physical input I was receiving, I heard voices telling me they loved me. I gasped out that I loved God. At that time, my sickness took a brief break and the weight of hallucinations lifted. I stood, and crawled in the window, and found the couch.

I sat on the couch, in a glowing room, wondering why I didn't die and if I was still going to die. I decided to try and live and so I called 911 and asked them to come and look at me because I thought I was dying.

When they arrived, the paramedics were confused. My heart rate and oxygen levels were normal and I wasn't dying. I guess Schizophrenia is really that strange.

Musings of a Schizophrenic Drunk

They talked to me, took me to the Emergency Room for observation because I told them about the dry heaving, and I wasn't intoxicated. I didn't explain about the demons; that was all going on inside of me in a way I couldn't explain. I was outwardly very quiet and I guess it felt good to be around people because after the trip to the Emergency Room and back in a free cab, I felt much less physical pain.

I didn't know what was going on. I still don't know why my behavior didn't have schizophrenia flashing lights all over it that night. Or, the next time I called 911.

The next time, I was home alone and fed up with all the cameras and bugs in the house. So, I called the police and when they arrived I asked them if they had the house under surveillance. They laughed at me, and said no. They left, and I was still upset because there were cameras all over the house driving me crazy.

It must be tough sometimes to tell a criminal from a crazy person, from a drunk. That was probably Phil's problem too in my final weeks before I went to the hospital. He'd stop by and I'd be clearly schizophrenic.

But, like the paramedics and the police he didn't really know what to make of my behavior.

I wish I hadn't been so angry with Phil. He could have maybe told me I wasn't acting quite myself, if I hadn't always run him off with waving arms and angry words, and maybe I could have gotten some help earlier and been hospitalized for fewer weeks. Once the psychosis sets in hard, the medication takes longer to quiet the mind. But, I was convinced he had locked me in a box with snakes for days early on in our relationship. I would try to argue with him about that when I saw him.

I'm pretty sure he had no idea what I was talking about or how to deal with someone so strange.

The delusions grew stronger and more intense. I was led to believe by the voices in my head that I was 10 years older than I was; that my real birth certificate had been destroyed; and that I had led a life secret of which I should be greatly ashamed.

I had, according to schizophrenic voices, been a famous porn star. The producers wanted me to quietly retire because I had too much dirt on a set of very powerful people. I was instructed to check my bank account and in it I would find 450 million dollars.

I was to leave the country with the money. Specifically, I was to fly to Italy and begin a new life under an alias. I began following instructions.

There was a voice that was going to meet me on the plane and accompany me to Italy. I went to the bank, fully intending to withdraw the money and go to the airport. Luckily, the account had only a balance of 50 dollars.

If I had been richer at that point in my life, I would have boarded a plane, in the throes of a psychotic break, for Italy. Instead, I drove home and the delusions continued to talk me awake for a few more days. They sent me on walking trips around town; they burst me into tears; they made my body ache; they convinced me I was dying; and they were always rolling the cameras that were hidden in the bookcase, above the backdoor, in the yard, in the bathroom, and in the TV set.

I was dying, I thought, so I made a will:

I, Woodsie T. Bunny, being of semi-sane mind and body, isn't everybody? I would like all my money to be spent in the following ways.

1.   *A foundation under the name **Woodsie Bunny Tree Foundation:** to be started by Fort Collins Arbor Services, especially planting new trees.*

2.   *Money to Bill O'Reily for his child abuse work*

3.   *All money from Original Cut Paper Art to Greta Van Sustren*

4.   *Money to Jodie Foster to donate to her favorite charity*

5.   *Money to Kurt Vonnegut- something to charity*

6.   *Money to John Nash for creative scientific research*

7.   *$ 10,000 Humane Society of Larimer county*

8.   *Fort Collins Parks and recreation*

9.   *Fort Collins Emergency Services*

10.   *Fort Collins Police and Fire department*

11.   *Tank of Gasoline and some matches for the burning and eradication of pornography: I'll light the match.*

12.   *"Take what you can," is what a pair of friends said to me, and isn't that true. I pass on that information to everyone not just the abused.*

Musings of a Schizophrenic Drunk

Unless otherwise noted, divide to money up equally between all parties and Greta Van Sustren gets all the money from original Cut paper art, except what I spend first, and please, Greta, have someone else do the work 'cuz you work hard enough. If Greta is unable fulfill her responsibilities, then give it all to the ATF association. They never helped me much, but they weren't overbearing.

I'd like to explain to each party in my will why I left them money, so there are no misunderstandings about how I feel now as I leave them money. But, I'll do that later 'cuz I ain't dead yet.

Living support of my body to be supplied only by natural and holistic methods: Body, mind, and soul.

Signed,

Woodsie T. Bunny

I guess I felt a special affinity for the newscasters because they were talking to me a lot telepathically during their newscasts, which I watched and gave them telepathic feedback on every night. The Fort Collins government made out good too in this will of mine. The presence of city vehicles made them ever active in my delusions as well.

Somehow, by the Grace of God, I believe, I ended up in the hospital before I got hurt. I clearly couldn't take care of myself, the hallucinations and delusions were relentless, and I was at great risk of putting my self in harm's way. How I really got there I don't know.

One day I took a cold cup of coffee and a warm container of milk, off a breakfast tray that another patient didn't pick up that morning from behind the nurses station, and sat at a table by a small window and imagined how things were.

Sippin' Sidewalk Cappuccino: Cold Coffee and Warm Milk

Musings of a Schizophrenic Drunk

She is sitting alone on a set of three wooden boards that are the seat of an old bench. The light is bright and temperature hot; the afternoon haze is rolling in off the oil slick harbor, lady liberty is still dirty and the children running home along the boardwalk don't notice her sippin' her coffee. They have moms waiting in their kitchens with snacks and advice. She pretends her empty cup and paper sack contain her dream. A stranger strolls by.

Me—got the time?

Sidewalk Stranger—No, why, what 'ya doing country girl? In this big city?

Me—sitting in my seat sippin' cold coffee and warm milk; it tastes like cappuccino to me.

Ss—why so slow?

Me—I'm waitin' for my man. He's tall and dark and sweet to me. 'Ya seen him downtown?

Ss—No, not there, not yet.

*Me—oh, well. His shoes are stolen, but the suit is his.
Change in his pocket, with no money to spend. He's got
a watch on a chain; forgot it at home. What time is it
anyway?*

Ss—Don't know, why?

*Me—Cause he pickin' me up for the big show, in the
building over there, it's posted on the park bench
between there and here.*

Ss—why don't you go by yourself?

*Me—I don't have a ticket. He's got our tickets. That's
why I'm sippin' so slow: I don't know when the show
starts*

*My man never rescued me off the wooden bench. A not
so brief stay in a psychiatric ward was court ordered, I
kept drinkin' coffee.*

*Me—I'm locked down in the mental hospital with a
broken heart.*

Musings of a Schizophrenic Drunk

Him—who broke it, country girl?

Me—Men mostly, and my mom and dad. They all say they love me now, but not like I'm like them.

Him—Like how do people love you half pint?

Me—They all think I'm sick, they care about me, they want to help me, and they call that love. So, that's what I'm in for: a broken heart.

Him—So sad. How'd it break again?

Me—Yep, once more. This time I landed here. When I loved them the way I knew and they couldn't feel it and they loved me the way they knew and I couldn't feel it, we all ended up confused.

Him—Me too, how could anybody not love you? Did your man not show up with the tickets and that's why your mind up and split?

Me—Something like that. I waited till long after my coffee was gone and the sun had set over the boardwalk. I couldn't cry and I got mad.

Him—some other kind of ride arrived?

Me—yeah, a big rectangular box with lights on top, a nice bed, and someone to talk to.

…TIME IN THE WARD…

Me—I'm getting out of here one day. Off I'll go, and, even though I'll be mostly alone, I'll still play.

Him—What will you play country girl?
Me—I'll play rock n' roll, bike rides at dusk, jokes to myself, and pick-up-sticks. I am moving on. So sorry, to myself, that I let it get me so down when my man didn't bring the tickets.

Him—Sounds real good. Can I come?

Me—You got tickets to the show?

Him—No.

Me—Well, just sit with me a while here then. No games though.

Musings of a Schizophrenic Drunk

Him—Just sit with you a while?

Me—yep.

Him—then what?

Me—maybe we could talk.

Him—about what country girl?

Me—I don't know, you're the guy.

--

--

--

--

Him—It is a beautiful sunset.

Chapter 10
Hospital Life

The hospital was.

And, I stayed longer.

I attempted to draw a flow chart to figure out how I had landed there. I had all kinds of issues like mental hospitals (that's were I was), jail (that is where judges had been telling me I was headed), and detox (that is what I had been avoiding) on my mind. Darkness and light seemed like the options for exiting this flow chart and I guess I wanted to figure the way to the light. I drew the chart on a piece of paper I got from the nurse's station.

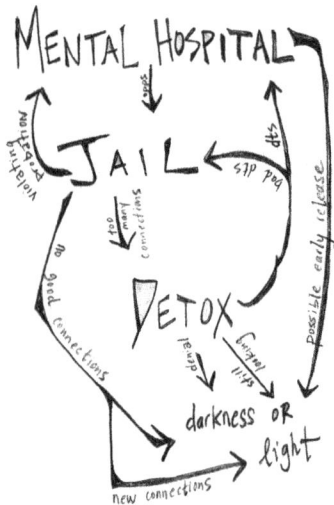

Musings of a Schizophrenic Drunk

The medication began to deaden the electrical impulses
sent by renegade neurons with a mind of their own.
And, I didn't sleep much.

Staff at hospital: We all feel tired sometimes
Me: You do?
Voices: We all feel tired sometimes but we can't sleep.
Staff at hospital: How about some warm milk?
Me: Yes, I'd like that.

A man, he was 6' 1" and a half, standing in the frame of
the doorway when he told me about his hand that day.
He offered me milk another night. I always appreciated
the milk because he broke the rule for me.

A number one rule in the hospital is "make 'um sleep."
Because when patients don't sleep long enough, they
get tired. Sleep is different on anti-psychotics. Real
sleep is different; I feel rested in my mind and body, my
mind is calm and doesn't jump away from my dreams
and let me forget. I remember my dreams.

Anti-psychotics knock me out. I wake up the next day
tired and drowsy. The pills only let my body rest; they

stop the electric jolts that bring schizophrenic delusions and violent visions but there is no sleep.

I wanted badly to heal hard and fast from my most recent psychotic break. I'd spent years, four, weaning myself from anti-psychotics and dreaded a drugged life where I never would sleep human sleep. I longed for the end of sleep time being less than knocked out time. I would be able to work and talk to people and have original thoughts.

When I was on anti-psychotics, I was trapped in exhaustion.

I'll never let go of the memory of the tall man in the door frame getting me warm milk to sleep. He broke protocol in the hospital and it helped me have more energy to think. The Lithium takes care of the energy when it gets too much. The warm milk helped me slip into a few moments of sleep better than another Haldol would have.

In my mind now, he was an especially strange candidate for this. He was in the doorway and it showed me his height. After telling me about how his hand was damaged badly from an inmate there in the mental hospital, he showed me his size and it explained the damage that can be done by crazed people like me. Yet, he gave me milk and encouraged me to try again at sleep instead of insisting on another pill.

I might have slept that night for a moment or two. I thought a lot about how the man showed me kindness and must have thought of me as a human being.

Another sleepless night I wrote this in the hallway. I'd sit in hallway at night with a blanket wrapped around me writing sometimes, reading sometimes. My roommate would be in the room and the lights would be out. Other patients would stop by my square of floor to talk when they were having sleepless nights.

What I have in common with truly insane people is (or maybe it's just me):

We can speak in normal tones with tears streaming down our faces about terrible memories, or we can cry about other terrible thoughts, or we can laugh out loud still crying, or we can sit still with tears rolling slowly from dry eyes, or we might do something else. And, we will think nothing of it except "that's what happened." Because we are not ashamed of feeling emotion and, unfortunately for the observers, letting emotions run free.

Right now, though, the only part of realizing that this describes me that feels good is the fact that, at least, it is not just me who is truly insane from time to time. The rest kinda' twists under my skin and makes the devil grin. So, I keep on prayin' and lettin' God win.

God wins every time the devil grins and I don't turn red, ball up my fists and pound the walls. The insanity is not the company I long to keep: all alone in my head never getting any sleep, and bright daylight hours slipping away from my reach. I do long for healthy hours and evening times with people I love, and goals reached. So, I will lie down again, empty my head, say 1 more prayer, and wait for sleep to come.

I prayed for mercy a lot at the hospital.

God, I will do this for you. Because you did so much for me. If I end up naked, frozen, not dead, in crusty snow,

Musings of a Schizophrenic Drunk

I will do this for you. What will I do now according to my Christian beliefs? I will carry on and act as circumstances arrive. I will believe in myself. I will, at times, take chances. I will embrace my mental illness and learn from it. I will not be angry. I will not speak much. I will protect my body. I will feed my brain. I will be open to goodness. Because you died for me, I will live for you the best I can.

Amen

Prayer and reading the Bible got me through much of my hospital stay. Nothing made sense in the hospital. The doctors asked me strange questions that seemed to have nothing to do with my problems; the other patients would sometimes talk to me about strange things; I didn't like the food, but I was getting fat; I had non stop auditory hallucinations that kept me guessing about when I'd get out and where I'd go. Prayer would help and bring me hope sometimes. I guess because God loves everybody, even sick people.

Strengthening my faith in Jesus Christ:
A writing

Amara Lorch

As I pass through life and my knowledge of God's teachings, laws, power, and glory deepens, so does my faith in Christ. The stronger my belief in God's will; the stronger my faith in Jesus Christ grows. He guides me deeper into the Lord's kingdom and I can embrace his glory in all its most powerful beauty.

Psalm 118
Trust in the Lord

James 1:20
A man's anger does not allow him to be right with God.

I guess I prayed so much because of the way the illness schizophrenia makes me feel.

Musings of a Schizophrenic Drunk

Schizophrenia and Hellfire

--*What are voices, Amara?*

--*Voices are people I know who speak from their hearts to my mind. The echoes of schizophrenia are demons in hell who want me to kill myself and join their team.*

--*How many times have you tried to kill yourself, Amara?*

Five or six or four, I think.

--*Not very good at it, are you?*

--*Well, usually I'm psychotic and drunk, so I don't think it out very well. All I have to say, really, is thank God I have not been successful.*

--*Why, Amara?*

--*It gives me more opportunity to forgive myself and others and love God and Jesus. I felt real close to hell one time when I almost died of sickness; not suicide. I was dry heaving and suffocated to the point of unconsciousness lying on the ground. I wasn't drunk or drugged, just tired I guess. I felt hell approaching and I managed to say, "I love God" when I felt people loving me. The hellfire on my chest eased, and I was able to drag myself to the couch. I sat with God's light glowing and forgave everyone and myself.*

--Then what happened, Amara?

--Just as every time I feel so good and close to God, it happens that life on Earth begins again. People do things that I resent sometimes, and it gives me new opportunities to forgive and release resentments. It is a lot of work just living.

Holy Bible, New Life Version

2Cor 4:7-9

We have this light from God in our human bodies. This shows that the power is from God. It is not from our selves. We are pressed on every side, but we still have room to move. We are often in much trouble, but we never give up. People make it hard for us, but we are not left alone. We are knocked down, but we are not destroyed.

The power of God lights us from the inside and we pass it all around.

Musings of a Schizophrenic Drunk

I was mentally tortured my entire stay at Pueblo State Hospital by my hallucinations and delusions. I begged for release because I believed the walls were what was making my soul hurt so bad. The walls and jailhouse feel of it all didn't help me feel better; thinking about and praying to God did. I was sick and in a sort of jail.

Chapter 11
Not Done Yet: Another Hospital

I was released from Pueblo State Hospital only to be sent to another psychiatric ward a few days later. The sickness wasn't gone even after a month long rest and all the medication they administered. The jolt of exiting the hospital and re-entering a life that was so confused set my mind back into strong psychosis. Or, maybe I never left it?

Phil had been calling me in the evening at the Pueblo hospital. It would calm me and make me feel connected to reality. He loves me and his love would make me feel human. He mentioned things like getting married, tree work, and seeing him when I got out. But, when I got out I didn't think to call him for a ride or find out where he was. I went home to locked doors and climbed in the window.

I remembered Phil, called him, and went to his place to wait for him to get off work. I was doing better than when I left. But, life on the outside sent the delusions into action. I was, once again, delusional and getting messages from voices that I believed were Phil talking telepathically to me. The telepathic messages worked strongly against what he was saying aloud to restore our relationship.

I believed that my true sickness was not being able to talk telepathically as well as everybody else. See, I thought people had been taught the ins and outs of human communication, which was telepathy, from the age out loud talking and listening began. Everyone, except sick people like me, could call up whom they wanted to communicate with and turn conversations off when they wanted to think to themselves.

My never ending, delusional fantasy played out the story of Phil having a telepathic lover throughout our entire relationship. Now that my brain had split open and I was beginning to be able to communicate like all humans, the voice playing Phil agreed to be completely with me. But he needed time to end his current telepathic relationship appropriately. I begged him to be completely with me from there on out, and explained that I loved him and needed him to help me learn telepathy. Only true learning to communicate could come from a true love since most humans were taught to communicate telepathically from the unconditional love of a parent.

Of course, the voices kept me very upset about Phil's telepathic lover. They played moments of their conversations in my brain and tore through trust I had in Phil. Phil would speak out loud to me in conversations a reunited couple might have. I could barely hear him through the messages my brain was sending me from his imposter.

What Phil did was be with me for all the relearning required after a bout with mental illness. He couldn't hear me pleading, in my head, for him to be with me completely. He just did it in real life without me understanding he was doing it.

I asked backwards and in my head, to voices that weren't Phil, for what he willing gave. I pleaded for the love and help he was already giving by talking and living with me. I was upside down and inside out and the forces inside my brain were so strong.

The only thing that hadn't changed was that schizophrenia was still weird. Phil thought I looked tired and was not quite me, but he didn't know that I still didn't understand the difference between an auditory hallucination and a telepathic message. The doctors hadn't pinned that one down either, 'cause they let me out. Maybe the staff and doctors should have asked me about telepathy and voices in more detail, so I'd be safe outside of the hospital and not screw up my life more. Instead, they observed me and observed me. You can't see schizophrenia.

In Mountain Crest, the next hospital, I stayed in the acute ward and mostly wrote down my delusions and read the Bible.

The Boundary of A Place

As I lay resting in my bed, I felt myself sinking into a terrible place. I saw a door opening across the room; blackness was there. I opened my eyes so I couldn't see that vision anymore. My body felt darkness and pain.

A few thoughts crossed my mind. I prayed to God as the waves of sadness rolled through. I realized that Phil never loved me. He wouldn't tell stories, ask if I was well, or send any love my way at all. That set into my body real good. I felt the cold electricity of hell.

Then I kept still with God; and I reached the boundary of a place I knew from before. They call this one heaven. It feels as if I don't need a body anymore when I reach this gate.

God lives above a wide open green meadow with no trees. When I go to him I gaze out towards the East. It is morning time.

My voices gained names and made up stories about how I had led a very terrible life. They tried to tell me at the end of this next delusional burst that I had schizophrenia, but I wouldn't listen or maybe I didn't understand what schizophrenia was at that point. I wish someone in the hospital would have explained what schizophrenia was to me. That mental health lesson coupled with this delusion might have been a good clue to head me on down a road to recovery.

Musings of a Schizophrenic Drunk

Psycho-sexual-abuse sleuth

I am a fractured soul with an illness. They called me schizophrenic at 28 years. Upon relapse, years later now, my fractured soul has the same disorder: schizophrenia make and model. A fracture is easy to heal when you know it's there.

We use stitches and glue. The stories we tell each other, inside my shattered skull, will pull us tight together. The bonded soul will be sealed with Elmer's glue so that one soul remains.

One soul remains with an illness, that's true. But, it is a lot less easy to pick on one than two, when schizophrenia is the case.

My split-brain took away all the pain from the sexual-psycho abuse. She is kind of nuts in a way, and still refuses to come out and fuse. She says the pain is too great the way things are and it's my turn, still, to soak up all the abuse. She was present for all that I can see except in cloudy sleep deprived memories.

Amara Lorch

*My suicide attempts tried to kill her too. I talk about this
with my split brain when I don't want her to get pissed
off, and up and split; leaving me in the dark. My split-
brain says, "Amara, why'd ya do that? You tried to kill
me too, I don't want to die Amara." So, as far as
stitches go, we have some work to do before she'll trust
me completely. And, me her too.*

*I named my split Ouch; she takes all the pain. Days
later she changed her name to Quick to account for her
wit. She has the same sense of humor as me, 'cause,
as the doctors tell me, she's me. And I guess that's why
she's like that. She's not that bad especially after all
that she's been through. I wonder about her
sometimes. How she'll do when we are one and not
two.*

*And, still, I did not cry, much. Even though, I was
feeling abused and overused. I am a fragmented soul.*

*What I remember from my childhood is nothing like it
was. I remember a photo I saw of my sisters using me
as a pillow. What happened God told me later through
repressed memories. I sat in my room a lot for being a
bad girl: wiping hands on my pants when I'd come in*

Musings of a Schizophrenic Drunk

from the barn. I didn't have any friends and my sisters
wouldn't play with me 'cause I was dirty. A few times,
my mom put straw in my bed and told me I was a dirty
pig, then still didn't tuck me in. I did not cry a lot. I was
not invited to dinner; told I was sick; fed from a tray in
my room; when actually I felt fine. I did not think a lot.

Later, when I'd pretend to be asleep, mom and dad
would come in and argue loudly over me and my bed.
Year two was empty of memories till I laid down 34
years later and I recalled some memories.

These are the stories Quick tells me, in my head, and
shows me images of and attaches feelings and
emotions to, while I sit silently still and ill in my hospital
room. Quick never stops talking, sending these images
that feel like memories, and making jokes.

Today, her name is "what-ya-got." She says it like a
joke on me for telling me all those crazy stories of abuse
that really did not occur. Turns out I am just crazy.
"What-ya-got is schizophrenia"; that is the joke on me
these days.

Sure, I believed all those repressed memories like they were things that actually occurred, wouldn't you? When hallucinations are so vivid and true, it is hard to know what to do. I was sure that abuse was the cause of my mental hospital stays.

I felt watched. In the hospital people shuffled by my door as they navigated the halls. One night, late, a scary man walked by and peered in at me. He told me through telepathy that he had raped me on the outside and he was coming back to rape me again. I felt scared and helpless, I didn't sleep that night.

There was a half circle on the ceiling above the door. A camera, I figured. I wondered where the monitor screen was.

And, then, of course, there was the portal to the world in my brain. Everyone was aware where I was. I mean everyone, from celebrities, to people I walked past in a store one day, to Nobel Peace Prize laureates, to the minister at church. We all talked a lot and I asked them to get me out of the hospital. They all said there was nothing they could do.

Musings of a Schizophrenic Drunk

Fishbowl

I live in a fishbowl. I've got a few different kinds of rocks and a pirate ship. I couldn't hear outside the bowl before, when they had a lid on the tank. A nosey cat knocked the lid off and now instead of silence, I hear the world. There is a kid in the house who throws rocks in the tank. The water squeezes my body.

Life would be better if they'd put my bowl on the window sill so I could see the view. The world is noisy, and I don't know what the sounds mean. Sometimes life for a fish is like that.

I don't like it when people walk by and look at me. I'm a fish, and I am not free. Strangers throw rocks gently at the glass; ping, ping, ping and I can't answer back.

I'm a fish.

I had a friend from the portal who I enjoyed talking with when he'd call. He was Papillon. He spent a long time in a French penal colony, and offered me lots suggestions to conquer boredom. He wasn't real impressed with the trial I was going through; it seemed he just enjoyed talking with me. He told me he was the toughest man in the world. I don't doubt that from what he's been through. Too bad, I can't talk to the real man.

Acute Unit: Two Days Left

My friend, Papillon, called me to talk when I had two days left in the Acute Unit. Two days turned into five because the paperwork got shuffled, or something like that.

Pap—Everyone asks me about the penal colony.
Me—Really not relevant, is it?
Pap—Really it…
Me---I don't like that relevant word, I guess it is…..
Pap---Overused and abused
Me--- (pause) I like you Pap, you're a cool cat.

We spoke again upon release. I always get a kick out of talking with Pap.

Musings of a Schizophrenic Drunk

Me—It's to better to ask forgiveness than permission,
but better than that…..
Pap—don't get caught
Me—Like the pen I stole in the hospital, Pap?
Pap—Kinda' like that
Me—where would I have been without a pen? I wrote
and it kept me calm when the hallway got too short.

Chapter 12
Out of the Hospital: Bills in the Mailbox

They let me out. Once again, I was deemed sane enough to be out of the hospital. And, it was hard to know what I would do. I'd lost my man, my job was a business we ran together, and I was still pretty sick. It was tough to figure my way. I managed to get to the fifth floor of a government building one day to apply for disability. Their eyebrows raised at me. 'You don't look disabled; how could you be disabled with such pretty hair.' That is what their looks made me feel.

I don't know if they thought that. Maybe they thought I looked real bad? I couldn't see their thoughts or feelings; just like you can't see Schizophrenia. I didn't like the errand. Being out in public around so many people made my heart race, head spin, I worried I'd get lost and not be able to find home, but I knew I needed money. People kept sending me bills. So, I applied for disability.

Musings of a Schizophrenic Drunk

The Future of Schizophrenia

Sometimes it pays to be crazy; I could do without the abuse.

I am back from my month long leave at the mental hospitality wards in this fine state of Colorado. My state is deteriorating rapidly. Sometimes people ask me what I will do to make money or survive. All I want to say is: aren't I? Aren't I alive?

But, it is never good enough to be just me when I appear so strange. I look like I'm laughing because of all the jokes inside. The things I do make people say, "How can you do that?" So, then they ask for much more and play games with me that I don't understand. They are mean games that mean nothing because what the say and do are on opposite sides.

I am left alone rarely; I cannot hear myself think. I do monotonous repetitive tasks to keep my mind alive. I really don't think I will ever be able to do anything again. I am dead. Then, I say to myself I'll just answer that call, and it leads me on. But, I'd like to make a few calls of my own today.

I'd like to be left in peace with friends (in my head friends) *to heal from the demons of Schizophrenia and split-brain syndrome. I am out here floating; in pain mostly.*

I prayed today. That made me feel good. I will do that more often.

Moving around town is difficult. I feel fear sometimes. I feel overwhelmed sometimes. Always, it makes me tired.

Before the hospital, I had endless energy coupled with psychosis. Now, I struggle to do things. But, I keep trying to get out and do things. The trip to apply for disability was a step toward healing. It challenged me and allowed me to feel where I was at and what was hard or easy. Then, I try something new and see what I can do.

Progress requires effort.

Quick: Amara, what do you think I'd look like if I was a person?

Me: Quick, please go think to yourself for a while, I'm writing.

Quick: Amara, it's important.

Quick: Really, really, really important.

Me: You'd look like a little kid, a fat little kid.

Quick: That's not nice. Why a fat little kid?

Me: Cause you're mean and pull my pigtails.

Quick: That's true.

Me: You've got no stress. You don't seem to care if I'm working, dying, in the hospital, whatever. As long as you have someone to talk to you're ok.

Quick: I don't have many worries, do I? But, what am I?

Me: You're a voice in my head. An auditory hallucination. You're not real.

Quick: Amara, remember when I had you look up voice in the dictionary?

Me: Yeah?

Quick: Well, I want a voice, I don't want to be a voice anymore.

You guys: Quick, when the book is published, you'll have a voice, ok?

Quick: Yeah, what I say is in the book, that's good. Let's publish it.

Me: Yes, you'll have a voice when it is published, Quick.

Quick: I know another reason to publish the book, Amara.

You guys: Why is that, Quick?

Quick: So Amara can get off disability.

You guys: Quick. She'll maybe make a buck or two on the job.

Quick: that's it?

You guys: Yeah, her parents will probably buy a copy of it.

Quick: I don't know, Amara, I think you are pretty messed up in the head for publishing a book.

Chapter 13
Getting Well

It is hard to say when psychosis ends and reality begins. The medication has a lot to do with that. It is a moment or a thousand moments that eventually find me in a place where I do not believe fantasies anymore. I look around and seeing is, once again, believing.

Phil visited with me in the hospital through real wires, an actual telephone. He called me after work everyday and his voice would calm me. He moved back in when I got home, and he has been loving me well ever since.

I was able to hear his voice and not the telepathy this time. We quit drinking together, forever. We wanted to be ourselves; and not live as sick shells, of human form, without conscience.

Slowly, I build myself again alongside my love who returned after his own journey to the depths of alcoholism. His journey didn't dip into a form of insanity that they can lock you up for, but he told me that his vista was dark and grim.

The brief separation brought true joy to me only upon reunion. I had found my friend again and now we shared a vision: life on sober terms where joy and anger live in separate camps. Here, we figure our emotions will make more sense and flow at smoother speeds.

Turning the corner

I prayed a lot of thanks today. How can I explain the wonderful feeling of voices and echoes leaving my mind free. The stories I have told explain some of what the sickness was telling me. The intensity is that I believed all of what they said.

I went to church today with Phil, and I could hear the sermon. The last two times I went to church, since my release from the mental hospital, my mind was so cluttered with voices and echoes that I couldn't decipher what the words said were.

Then, I sat and listened to the wind and the birds.

Then, I watched TV amazed that the newscasters were not talking to me.

Musings of a Schizophrenic Drunk

It all happened so fast. After months of delusions and hallucinations, suddenly I was thrust back into reality. I don't know how it happens for other schizophrenics, for me it was as soon as I stopped believing the delusions that accompanied the auditory hallucinations the hallucinations stopped their constant onslaught.

Now, I just have to get back in shape and deal with the alcoholism as I manage Schizophrenic symptoms. Sounds easy? I will go help lift logs into a trailer today for a while, till I get too tired. And, Phil and I are together and helping each other stay sober. We have been thinking together silently and aloud; the drinking was the cause of our crazed fights.

Last night, we said to each other in bed, "When we drink the same things we talk about now, like this, make us angry." I feel so grateful to not have lost Phil in the course of months of psychosis and a few years of too much drinking. I believe the heavy drinking caused the psychosis. And, it didn't do Phil too much good either.

We are committed to staying sober and healthy together.

Together again, and occupying the same space we did during the drunken years. Strange, especially coming out of my psychotic haze, to learn to do the things we do again. "I know I like doing this, I am enjoying myself, and I wonder what to do with myself now."

Not having to go and get a beer from time to time leaves me with some scheduling difficulties. We talk about how it is: either drink or live. Drinking leads to jail cells and mental wards for us. We love each other; we are learning to do what we do again, together.

Working in the shop is different now. When I don't have something to do, it is harder to just stand there and talk. Before we'd work, talk and drink for a few hours. Then, when we were wondering what do, we'd go on a beer run. Then, hours would pass until the day was done. Now, I find myself pacing more, moving inside to write and do my artwork, think about dinner, and dragging enjoyable tasks out for longer times.

Slowly, learning to not drink. Slowly, rebuilding my brain.

Musings of a Schizophrenic Drunk

Seems to be working better for me than getting arrested. I must have been a little psychotic when I thought that the arrest was a good thing. I am happy now because I am rebuilding my strength, and Phil and I are together again. This is what I wrote when I was arrested, psychotic, seemingly gleeful at the thought of probation. I don't really like the probation without the psychosis. It is different now than then:

If my legal case continues on the path it is currently on, it looks like getting arrested worked out pretty good for me. I am still free. The long hallways filled with people in slippers, who are filled with sedatives, is not home to me. I am getting freer. The relationship I am ending is untying its logistical knots; a little more each day.

Nothing is fair. I think about that as a concept at times. I experience it the most when I want something. For example, I want the charge to be dropped, my record forever expunged, and maybe a cookie with frosting and a smiley face on top. It looks like the charge might very well stick. That cookie crumbled.

Maybe it will still taste good if I sprinkle it on top of ice cream and drizzle chocolate sauce on top. Then I could just smile when I explain my criminal charge to potential employers. I'm sure they will be very interested in the whole story and probably think that an event like that, and the clean up following, has deepened my character and then they would decide to make me team leader. Or, at least, it could put a smile on their face.

Guess I'll be finding out more about that in this life.

Chapter 14
Legal Troubles Remain

I got myself arrested one night, during the time Phil and I were splitting up, by resisting a few police officers as they tried to tell me I was crazy and walk me into an emergency room. I talked my way out of the hospital and landed in jail with an obstruction charge.

I did not want to be headed for the mental hospital. I didn't see it coming, and fought it the whole way. I thought jail or probation would be better than sickness. So, I told the police, "I don't have Schizophrenia; I am just crazy". They believed me that night and put me in jail.

It wasn't a choice I could make. The judge judged me guilty. I accumulated a charge. And the illness grew stronger even with the legal troubles. A month later, I was in the hospital.

The cookie, well that never came. Everything is a little bit realer now: alcohol classes, 20 days alternative sentencing to be served, and lots of money required by the government. All the legal consequences waited, patiently, for me to get out of the hospital.

I guess my judgment was a little off during the time I approached my stays at the mental wards here in Colorado. I just move along, cleaning up my mess a little at a time.

Chapter 15
Life Goes on at Home

We are back where we were when we met. Phil is out in the yard beating his knuckles on greasy engines and I am at his side, but, once again, my mind is on brain structures. I am enjoying the evening shade on a hot August day and talking quietly with Phil as he removes a leaking radiator from a big, white, gas-guzzling truck.

My mind is on brain structures. I don't talk about it because the empirical stuff is the important stuff these days: what is out where we can see it and touch it. Although Phil does not like his knuckles being the things to touch the reality around us, his efforts and work draw me into the world. I am involved in the project, and less and less I wonder why my brain still talks to me in jokes and sarcastic remarks about mistakes I've made and plans I have.

The comments, from my sickened brain structures, get fewer and farther between. Phil says something and I hear him completely. I am happy.

It is also, about our love, a wonderful evening. It has been four years now, and we have struggled through a lot of it against alcoholism and mental illness, and we are still here together. If we would have made fewer mistakes, maybe we would not be so broke and still be trying to start a business and get financially stable, but I wouldn't love him any more than I do now.

As he unglues stuck bolts with cheater bars, I gather dry seeds from a Penstemon perennial we bought the other week. It blooms June through August in bright purple flowers up and down its stalks. I plan to sow the seeds in the front of the house this coming spring. I tuck the seeds away in a dry place, and Phil listens as I tell him about it.

Springtime is the season for planting seeds.
New growth and letting go of winter's tragedy.
I will let go of yesteryear's failed crops now.
I may or may not plant a new crop,
But I will not dwell on the fruit that crop did not yield.
Warm weather melts the snow from inside me.

His support throughout my recovery since the hospital has been this simple and wonderful the entire time. He believes I will come back fully as myself in mind and body; he waits for me; he does things with me that draw me into life and out of painful internal confusion that is bouncing about inside my gray matter; and I guess all he has to do is be himself.

I am not complete in what I can do compared to what I think I want to be able to do. I tire easily and retreat to rest before I have done half of what I could do before. I am discouraged at times. Phil's support, at these times, is crucial. He doesn't claim to understand what a 'voice' is; rather, his advice is "keep going," "do things that make you feel good," "I know you'll be well soon." And, I can make myself take another step.

He doesn't know I'm thinking all this right now. He is a man working on a truck. I stand here holding a light on his work and hope he at least knows how much I love him and how his love helps me heal. So, I tell him I love him a lot.

Recovery from schizophrenia, the type I have, is slow, painful at times, cluttered thoughts, anxiety, and thick mud in my path. I have a lifetime to get through it; until the end of all that, I will enjoy the parts I can.

Chapter 16
Personal Progress

Writing a book about my hard times seems like a strange way to pass the time. But, I chose to do it. And, it helps me heal. My hope is that someone, suffering with schizophrenia or alcoholism, or both, will read this memoir of mine and gain hope of a future after illness and a speedy recovery.

A month or so before I entered the Pueblo State Hospital, I was reading Slaughter House Five. I was in the bathtub, psychosis was strongly seeping into my brain, and I was reading one page over and over again. Although I was not absorbing the content of the book, I got something from the experience. When I flipped to the back cover and read a little about Kurt Vonnegut, I was surprised to see his writings described as Schizophrenic.

Kurt Vonnegut didn't have schizophrenia. I interpreted the biography to mean that he did. Phil was still at home and I hopped onto the couch next to him after my bath, read him a passage, and told him how it gave me

Musings of a Schizophrenic Drunk

hope that a man with schizophrenia could be a successful author and lead a full life. I thought about that conception of mine during my recovery and it gave my strength to keep writing, thinking, and believing that I would be of one mind again; not caught in a split between reality and delusions.

Well, who ever is reading my book now can be sure: I do have schizophrenia and I did write a book. And, I have done more than that since I got out of the hospital:

I began to work as an arborist again, slowly, with the love and support of my Phil; I am doing my cut paper art and hope to brighten the world with it someday; and I am sober and able to maintain a loving relationship.

I still hear voices, but I am not in a delusional state. Who knows how long these hallucinations will linger in my consciousness? I do know that I will not be burdened by them; I will continue to put my stock in the empirical world around me and grow within it.

Chapter 17
Home Detention

It is nice that you all read this book. It would be nice if it was over at the end of the last chapter, but my healing goes on and even speedy recoveries take time. Joy is sometimes still hard to feel, I have to talk myself into taking a step or two, and my faith in God is, at times, all that lets me truly believe that anything is worth doing on this Earth.

So, I'm in home detention now. The doctor's said jail wouldn't be good for me, the police hadn't forgotten about me breaking the law, and home detention was the option the judge thought fit best. 36 days of an ankle monitor that detects my presence in the home. When I'm out and about at permitted activities, all my location changes must be reported by calling into Work Release Headquarters.

Pretty simple life really. On the outside.

Here is a sample of how this simple life, on the outside, sounds to me.

Me: (dial phone.)

Work Release (WR): Work release, this is Christine.

Me: Lorch.

WR: Yeah?

Me: I'm headed to 1600 North College.

WR: ok.

Me: (disconnect phone)

I drive to the bank to deposit money so Phil and I can pay our yearly fee to update the legality of our LLC. I arrive.

Me: (dial phone)

WR: Work Release, this is Christine.

Me: Lorch, 1600 North College; that's where I'm at.

WR: Thanks.

Me: (disconnect phone)

I enter the bank. My heart begins to race. I don't know why. It makes me feel dizzy.

Quick: Amara.

Quick: Amara.

Me: What Quick?

Quick: I have a location change.

Me: Do it right Quick.

Quick: Ring, Ring

Me: Amara , work release.

Quick: This is Quick

Me: Yeah, what?

Quick: I am headed to the Medulla Oblongata.

Me: ok.

I converse with the teller in order to get the money in the bank. He is friendly; I am friendly. I return to the truck.

You guys: Quick what are you doing?

Quick: I am telling Amara that I am going to the Medulla Oblongata.

You guys: Why? Do you even know where that is?

Quick: No, I have no idea where it is, do you guys know?

You guys: It is near the brain stem Quick, do you think you can find that?

Quick: I can't see anything in here with all these neurons in my way. I'm not really going there anyway; I couldn't slow Amara's heart, I don't know how. I just tell her that to make her feel better. She's crazy you know, so it does calm her a bit.

Musings of a Schizophrenic Drunk

You guys: ok

Me: (dial phone)

WR: Work release, this is Jennifer.

Me: Lorch, I am headed to 1805 North College.

WR: What is at that location?

Me: A laundry mat.

WR: ok

Me: (Disconnect the phone)

Quick: Ring, ring.

Me: Amara, work release.

Quick: This is Quick. I need to report a location change.

Me: Go ahead.

Quick: They aren't that nice to you Amara, do it right.

Me: yeah, what?

Quick: I am headed to the Frontal Lobe.

Me: ok

Me: (dial phone)

WR: Work release this is Jennifer.

Me: Lorch.

WR: yeah?

Me: I am at 1805 North College.

WR: ok (phone disconnects)

I unload the climbing ropes from the back of the truck and prepare to wash years of dirt and grime from them.

You guys: Why the frontal Lobe quick?
Quick: Amara might need some help with the machine loading and change counting. So, I'm going to stimulate her frontal lobe.
You guys: Really quick?
Quick: Nah, I can't really. I don't know how to do anything.
You guys: you're a good talker though Quick.
Quick: I have no response to that.

Quick: Amara, amara, amara...

I think I washed the ropes. I can't remember if I answered Quick that time or not. It all gets fuzzy. I'm just trying to keep the in's and the out's separate.

It makes me tired.

Me: (dial phone)
WR: work release, this is Christine.
Me: Lorch, I'm headed home.

WR: ok

Me: (disconnect phone)

Drive.

Me: (Dial phone)

Quick: Amara..

WR: Work release, this is Christine.

Me: I'm Home.

Quick: Amara….

WR: ok

Me: (disconnect the phone)

At home, I am letting the ropes dry on the floor of the living room. I can't wait to climb a tree again one day. I won't have to call in to let them know I'm in a tree, Quick won't have something to say, and I will feel the still focus of the swaying limbs.

The trip to the bank and laundry mat left me in the fetal position for an hour or two when I got home. I searched for a place inside of me where I could not hear anything inside or out. It wasn't really like resting. I got up. Slowly. Like I will do again. And again.

Progress requires effort.

Chapter 18

Progress Requires Effort

Progress requires effort.

"What do you mean by that?" something a paranoid schizophrenic might ask.

So, I say to you, "Please do, and let me explain."

There are many kinds of effort needed to produce progress in my recovery from a long term psychotic break. The first kind of effort is an effort to maintain the outlook that I will not be sick forever and that moments of success are worth the work. Anyone, who has been diagnosed with an incurable mental illness such as Schizophrenia or an incurable mental default such as alcoholism, can understand that general opinions of science and culture encourage resignation.

I can accept that I have limitations because of these illnesses, but I cannot accept that I "am" forever sick. This would work against my plan to get better. I am limited that I cannot drink anymore due to my alcoholism. I am limited by my schizophrenia symptoms in other ways. These limitations are not a defeat. They are challenges; they are opportunities; they are possibilities.

My limitations caused by schizophrenia offer me the opportunity to design a life that keeps demonic voices, unreal thoughts and beliefs, and anxiety at bay. I make the effort to perceive my life as a success, even if changed, every moment those symptoms do not surface.

As I work the best I can, struggling against a lethargy and a weight in my body that I did not know before the illness manifested earlier this year, I put out a second effort to maintain a clear perspective of reality by focusing on the task at hand.

I am lucky because I am aware, now, of the nature of my illness; I have some distance from the delusions and corrupt thought patterns that overtook my brain and landed me in a psychiatric ward.

I get tired quickly because I have to exercise my brain, at the same time my body is working, to keep my thoughts centered on the outside world and not floating about in fantasy. Circling thought patterns surface easily when not put into check. I work just as hard as I work in the trees, if not harder, in my brain to keep my mind quiet. When I need to rest, I sit quietly in the truck and meditate on objects like a tree or a steering wheel. These are objects that are outside of my brain, in the real world around me, but require no planning or reasoning. It rests my brain when thinking and being focused outside my brain is too much and my brain chain begins to skip. Sitting still and meditating on objects, forces my thoughts to dwell outside my body, but it does not overload my brain's work and my brain chain can run smooth and steady.

I work. I rest. I work at resting. I make it through a day and hopefully I strengthened my brain.

Throughout the course of my most recent schizophrenic episode, from initial paranoia, to silent delusions, to extreme hallucinations both auditory and visual, to my return to reality, to management of strange symptoms, I have an unusual awareness of my illness. Most people with schizophrenia have little perspective on the grid work of their illness. I described what being ill felt like to me. But, this book does not only dwell on my trip through illness; it journeys into being well again.

I notice that the problems I face today are rooted in the more severe symptoms of schizophrenia. A general underlying feeling, rooted in thoughts, of not being able to let go of things that worry or upset me, disturbs my brain's ability to function at its highest level. In deep psychosis, I got so upset that I would have strong physical reactions to this upset, like vomiting and extremely high heart rates. These physical manifestations were caused by my thoughts. They were delusional thoughts, but still just thoughts. They became untrue beliefs in many cases. Now, my decreased ability to concentrate and articulate is a result of renegade thoughts inside my brain's gearing system. The renegade thoughts are subconscious or silent sprockets operating on their own, stealing my brain's power.

My subconscious uses thoughts to keep me away from being fully engaged, or 100% on the outside. I noticed this today working with Phil. He was explaining to me what he was doing with the chipper (a machine we use to chip logs into mulch after we take limbs out of trees.).

As you can imagine, a brief run down of a mechanical project, like replacing a bearing in the guts of a chipper, is a series of short sentences comparing one part in relation to another and how they work together. "Loosen this one for that." "Better tight." "It's broken." "Can't move that without this."

These phrases make room for code talk to be heard by my brain when my subconscious is overactive. "It's broken," can refer to Phil saying the foundation of humanity is broken and he thinks the world is coming to an end. The simple meaning, as he points to a broken bearing, that the bearing is broken, is mixed in with a powerful stream of thoughts wondering (thinking in worse cases) why he is thinking about the end of the world. "I wonder if Phil is really worried about the end of the world and just scared to talk about it out loud, or if the bearing is just broken? Why would he be thinking about the end of the world?"

Quick: Amara, you're usually worried he is talking about the end of your relationship. Like he is breaking up with you or something.
Me: I was just using a non-personal example. I think they get it.

Musings of a Schizophrenic Drunk

Quick: Why do you think that stuff is coming out in code?

Me: That's it, Quick, I've cracked the code.

My sub-conscious is overactive. When I hear code it is pretty much always refers to past delusions. I don't hear code talk nearly as much now. In the depths of illness, everything I heard, or overheard, was referring to me and my delusions. And, I was convinced, by a strong belief, that the code talk was truly people telling me about what was really going on.

Now, when people talk around me, I hear phrases, and at times, I think, "Are they thinking about that too? They couldn't be." And, I force myself to push the thoughts out of my head and only hear the empirical meaning of the phrase.

I am learning to understand code phrases at just the right time. My overactive subconscious causes me unhappiness at times. I am carrying around unfinished thoughts in my head and not letting my subconscious clear. I can do something about this now.

This is the same subconscious that can be so strong, when it is operating at full strength, to alter my perspective of reality. Now, it just causes me feelings of worry deep down, even when I'm not aware of the thoughts. I can't let joy and love in completely.

I believe the two experiences, (1) the code talk I hear, and (2) being dragged down by things I don't even know I am worried about, both stem from my subconscious.

My brain is like an 18 speed mountain bike. How do I get it to run smoothly again? Three sprockets in front and six in the back are what run my brain. I need my brain chain to run across the gears so my thoughts flow smoothly and ideas always follow a progression where small ideas can grow to big and back again.

So, I must crack the code talk code. This may help me in more ways than one. It comes from sub layers of activity in my brain. I know that parts of my brain are sprockets spinning out of control when the chain is not engaged. When my brain chain jumps to those sprockets my thoughts jump to conclusions. When conscious thought, the running chain, shifts to a sprocket, that has been spinning independently, I am thrust into a developed thought that I did not develop.

As it stands now, I have a few sprockets that spin randomly, without the chain driving them, and my chain skips from gear to gear without my control at times. When my conscious thoughts or the chain I'm running, skips to a spinning sprocket without me trying to think in that gear, it causes problems.

Now that I got that figured out, I guess I'll start praying. Because I can't think of a way to fix that.

God, please let my chain run smooth on the gears I am thinking of consciously. And, please let the sprockets in my brain that run the bad, silent thoughts stop spinning. Amen.

I don't know if God feels that that would be the best thing for me right now. But, I can work on my brain chain a little bit on my own. God rewards those who try, right? Anyway, I gotta' try something.

I notice my brain feels good when I am fully engaged in an activity. Let's call that a low, strong gear. So, when the chain is on a powerful sprocket combination, or gear, chugging right along at a fairly steady rate, I feel good, clear, and focused.

There are quite a few useful sprocket combinations in my brain. Scientists have studied them and named them according to the roles they play. I'm not talking about the math sprocket compared to the reading sprocket. But, rather the levels of gears in my sprocket assembly that are empirical, abstract, fantasy, silent thoughts spinning in my subconscious, delusional, and other types of thought.

My delusion sprocket was all my chain rode on for many months. That one is not spinning today; it is wiped out, rusting in a corner. Keeping the low gears active will wipe out my quiet subconscious thought sprockets as well.

These are my gears. The lower the gear the stronger the calming force it has on my brain when I run my brain chain in that gear. The higher gears, well, their effect on my brain is disorder and chaos.

    1- (lowest, most powerful) God

Musings of a Schizophrenic Drunk

2- Manual labor/ Action

3- Planning a step by step task

4- Figuring out how to fix something

5- Reading

6- Abstract reasoning

7- Imagination

8- Making something imagined real

9- Making something real better

10- Looking forward to something

11- Memories

12- Silent circling worries

13- Silent circling worries

14- Voices

15- Silent circling worries (example: what do people think of me?)

16- Silent circling worries

17- Silent circling worries (example: thinking about some problem you can't fix at that moment like being in jail or on probation or paying too many taxes)

18- (highest, weakest) Delusions

    a. Emotions

    b. Feelings

The sprockets in my brain are not ordinary sprockets, and the chain is no ordinary chain. Instead of oiling the hub and chain when I have jumping, irregular thoughts, or reaching in to put it back together if the chain breaks when I am catatonic and just not thinking, I have to train the chain's electrical impulses. Because my brain, like most of them out there, runs an electrical chain. I'm not an electrician, but I feel that a steady, low pulsing chain on consciously engaged gears will help calm the spitting jolts that fire off the high gears in my brain causing me pain and discomfort. The high gears spin, even when my brain chain is running on a low gear, breaking my concentration with electrical shocks. These concentration breaks get fewer and further between the more I run the low gears. It takes a lot of time and effort to run in my low gears.

This is how it works in practice. My brain chain begins to skip sprockets. It is skipping to gears that store thoughts about things that make me uncomfortable and confused. "Time to throw it in low gear, Amara." I tell myself to find my strongest gear and I focus on God. "What a beautiful day you have created." I think only of the blue sky and low, light strips of clouds.

Musings of a Schizophrenic Drunk

Creator of all things. Always looking over me and all things. Always looking over me. He knows exactly what I'm doing, feeling and thinking. Because Jesus lived as a man, he knows exactly how I feel. And, all of me can handle everything in my path because God never gives you more than you can handle. Always looking over me. Great Job, Lord. Great Job.

The clouds. The blue sky. The sounds around me.

I keep it in low gear as long as possible. My chain stops skipping. I am rebuilding my brain. Training it to run steady.

Great Job, Lord. Great Job. I'm right here Lord. Thanks for looking over me.

Gear2: Manual Labor/ Action
Second gear is important to run, not only to train the electrical currents of my brain, but also a well tuned 2nd gear makes self sufficiency possible. This gear is all about doing. There are lots of things to do.

The trick for me, since I am training a brain that likes to short circuit, is maintaining concentration. I engage 2nd

gear by doing a variety of things. Some are good at keeping the gear running longer, some only allow short periods of clear running in 2nd before my chain skips to a higher, less efficient gear.

When I buck up fire wood, the adrenaline and fear of being injured run my brain chain low and hard. I rarely feel my chain skip until I feel physically tired and crave rest.

Gear 3: Planning a Step by Step Task

In gear three, planning a step by step task helps me pull my chain out of irregular skips in my high gears. When I don't have the strength to do, or I don't have the clarity to know what to do, I can slowly draw out steps in my head for a constructive project. Not constructive as in accomplishing a lot, but building something.

Driving home, I feel overwhelmed by the emptiness of the space and lack of motivation to craft that space; electrical jolts draw my chain into the weak, high gears. "I will build a sandwich in my brain now. Bread, lettuce, tomato, mayo out of fridge....." Although the details of the plan may not be necessary to sketch out for success, I do it anyway to occupy my brain space with low, steady pulsing brain chain and the high gears are disabled.

I get home and decide to do something else and eat a sandwich later with chips.

Gear 4: Figuring Out How to Fix Something
Gear four is easy to stay in when the thing I'm fixing is something I really want to work. I really want my brain to work.

Gear 5: Reading
As my efforts reap progress, my ability to run gear five improves.

Gear 6: Abstract Reasoning
What's that?

Gear 7: Imagination
When I first was re-entering reality a while back, I felt scared to use my imagination. It felt like imagination could slip into unreal delusional thought. Now, I love my imagination. It keeps me away from higher, more

destructive gears, and it can run a long and steady if I imagine the right stuff.

Gear 8: Making Something Imagined Real
When I write, I am making something imagined real. When I build a bench or table I am making something imagined real. This gear feels good to me. I can't run it non-stop because I need to take breaks and rest.

Gear 9: Making Something Real Better
I like having a gear that is designed solely to improve what I have done. The more I run my brain chain on this sprocket combination the better.

Gear 10: Looking Forward to Something
Now, the gears are getting higher. Anticipation, even if it is positive, is a gear I run sparingly. My brain chain is drawn to higher, sparking gears when I run gear ten for too long.

Gear 11: Memories
The memory sprockets are beautiful and terrible, both. I don't want to disable them, but better to wait till my brain

chain, conscious thought, is more under my control before I run this gear. Memories have a tendency to be filled with emotions and feelings that can make a fragile chain skip. I run this gear cautiously for now.

Gears 12,13,15,16, and 17: Silent Circling Worries

The silent circling worries, or subconscious activity in my brain is a problem if my brain chain is running on these gears or not. These sprockets spin at such high speeds that they shoot electrical currents all around my head. The faster they spin; the stronger the currents; the more attracted my brain chain is to them.

It seems one of my sprockets in this area of gears spins, on and on, about what people think of me. I noticed some "would be code talk" the other day waiting in line at the grocery story. If I was delusional, I would have believed the people were talking about me. That day, I just felt awkward and uncomfortable feelings. I combated them by explaining to myself it was just the spinning high gear that made me feel that way as it drew in emotions and feelings from underlying spinning thoughts about people's opinions of me. And, I had no empirical reason to feel any different than just fine. This sprocket produces a strong current. I can tell because it derails my brain chain and hooks it into useless paranoid thoughts. I threw it into gear two and just waited in line: action gear. I am working to disable gear fifteen. My work involves not shifting to that gear and working the low gears to make them stronger and more powerful.

All the silent circling worry gears function in the same manner. They all pick a different useless and damaging theme to spin about. The work is to identify their theme, not shift to that gear, and work the low, strong gears.

Gear 14: Voices
What to do about voices? Don't call out to them; don't answer them; don't have conversations with them; strengthen other gears.

Gear 18: Delusions
Delusions need as much external negative reinforcement as possible. Statements, by people that the sick person trusts, that discredit the validity of the delusions are this negative reinforcement. This is because the sick person is receiving non-stop positive reinforcement that the delusions are real from gears 12 through 18. To make matters worse, the 18th gear

whose sprockets combine to form delusions, when the chain drives on them, are reinforcing themselves with their spinning sub-sprockets of emotions and feelings.

With all those gears spinning to reinforce the delusional thoughts, a lot of negative reinforcement is needed externally.

Doctors, nurses, loved ones, and friends can all speak these truths to the sick person. They can even provide physical evidence or proof. First, they must find out what the delusions are.

When the delusions are discredited, in the sick person's mind, then the sick person can begin to have perspective. "If that's not true, what is really going on? Am I sick? What is true?"

With the code talk code cracked, and all my sprockets identified, I can now work on healing. Instead of feeling bad when "would be code talk" draws my brain chain to the high gears, I have a job to do. I run a low gear hard and steady, and try to identify the sprocket causing the problem so I can avoid shifting to that gear consciously. This puts me in gear two; I am doing. I do not just absorb the bad feelings and let them bring me down as they weaken my brain spinning my high gears. I strengthen my brain.

And, God heals me.

Chapter 19

God, Faith, and Healing

Raking leaves on a still day. Raking leaves reminds me of my faith in God. God might bring in a strong gust of wind and clean everything up completely. God does everything, you know. I keep raking. I keep raking and thinking about my body's motion and the pattern of leaves on the ground to train my brain to run in smooth circuits. God is wonderful, he heals me everyday and he could bring a strong wind, at any moment, to clean up all the leaves. I keep raking. And, soon, the ground is clear and the grass free to grow. Faith requires effort 'cause some jobs God doesn't want to do all by Himself.

Chapter 20
The Prayer I'm Looking For

The prayer I'm looking for will ask for protection. I have a long time to live before I die, and even though I feel fine now, I fear another day of psychosis. I don't know what words to use or even what to ask for in my prayer. I am scared of ways I felt and things I did when not in touch with reality. I tried to kill myself and I felt a rage towards others I'd never experienced before. Now I pray that I will call a hospital before I ever consider hurting my self or another human again.

It seems to me that being so ill that I am not interacting with the world around me is like dying. So my prayer is about not losing myself and my peace even in death. When I am lost and the world is not real, I'd like to still be myself at least in the way that doesn't hurt myself or others. I am scared to know this kind of death again. What happens when I am sick? How can I not lose control of a will to be peaceful? Now I pray for clarity in every moment.

And, I pray for guidance.

Chapter 21
Volunteering at Church

Ten fingers. Ten toes. Two legs. Two arms. One neck. A head full of rocks. I take inventory of my body in front of myself. All my parts are connected properly and I feel physically good. I'd like to paint the rocks in my head with brilliant colors to reflect the awesome world around me.

I am living on a disability check for the next three years, at least, due to the jackhammers that rattled my rocks this past year. The security of knowing a sum of money is coming in each month to pay bills allows me the comfort I need to exercise and strengthen my brain. I juggle ideas of how to spend my time.

I am alone most of my days when Phil is at work. I feel overwhelmed, most of the time, by the rattling rocks in my head. I feel a variety of mental health symptoms at a variety of times as I trip along in my days. Solitude takes me to place where I can feel lonely or full of love. Lack of distractions leaves too much time to feel. What I want to do is heal.

I need to be around people to rebuild my brain, but working is impossible for me now. I am on disability for a reason. I can manage my symptoms somewhat well, but I can not make them go away. Volunteering seems like a good way to give and get. I will be around people. Hearing their voices and ideas will be my escape from isolation and internal stimulus. I will give them the same.

During my sickest days, I found strength and comfort in the Lord's words when I read the Bible. I read them to myself silently and sometimes aloud to other sick people in the hospital. I'd like to do more of that. But, I am not in the hospital and I have no one to read the Bible with now. Hmmm…. How does one go about reading the Bible with others?

I went down to a local church the other day and filled out a form to volunteer. I stopped by again a few days later to follow up on the written request to donate time. I hope for an interview soon to discuss my desire to spend time with people in tough situations reading and discussing the Bible together.

Musings of a Schizophrenic Drunk

I'd like to bounce the idea of visiting female folks in jails and having Bible reading sessions. I imagine there would be all kinds of rules and regulations from the jail staff and the ministry. Yet, I dare to envision a small group setting where we all flip through the Bible and read our favorite passages to each other. The ladies would have plenty of time in their cells to pick out passages for the group, and I would be able to do the same at home with my free time.

It says in the Bible to pray for the people in prison. Better yet, I could pray with the people in jail. I'd go a few times a week, say two, for an hour and we would read aloud to each other from a very good book. I think that would help my own healing and possibly be of some good to the ladies in jail.

My interview with the volunteer department is continually being pushed back. And, I doubt they have "reading Bible in jail" as a regular volunteer activity. When I finally get in touch with someone at the church to talk about volunteer opportunities, I am thinking logically enough to not mention the jail time reading group. Of course, I feel awkward and out of place sitting in the church and asking to help in some fashion for free. I designed a simple plot to explain my way out of a line of questioning that might lead to talking about my mental illness.

It is the off season from tree work and business is slow. I am interested in doing something useful with my time until spring to keep busy. When spring comes, if I am still in need of milder physical activity with a more flexible time schedule, I can invent another reason for volunteering. The off season from tree work excuse will suffice for the entire winter. Since, I actually am an arborist it gives me something to talk about with people if they ask about my life. People like talking about what kind of work you do, and people like talking about trees.

It is good to have some kind of outline, of who you are going to present yourself as, when you go into an open situation. In my case, I find it extremely helpful because my mind too often wanders to the struggles I am having with my subconscious and I am tempted to talk about my illness, recovery, and struggles in general.

I am volunteering to distract myself from the trap of thinking only of getting well and not being sick. It is hard to grow myself in new directions, away from my illness, if I don't fill spaces in my mind with new things and grow them. Growing new experiences bonds my jack hammered rocks with new mortar.

That's where I'm at when I take on this new challenge of volunteering at the church. I am seeking mortar to stick my jagged rocks back together. I am constantly on the lookout for brightly colored paint to finish the job when these shards of rock become stones again. I just quietly put the paint colors in a safe place when I find them and I will paint them later, or as I go, when a smooth stone is formed.

On Tuesdays, I begin showing up at the missions department to help assemble reading glasses. The missionaries travel to needy neighborhoods and distribute the glasses. I feel good about the work. Poverty and homelessness are situations that some of the glasses recipients are dealing with in their lives. I am glad my efforts of cutting and sanding lenses contribute to pairs of glasses that allow someone dealing with these kinds of tough times to read the Bible or another good book. Isn't reading great?

Some days I wake up and have such a useful, productive list of things to do at home I wonder if going to volunteer at the church is a good idea. Couldn't I get more work done at home that would help the tree business or household organization?

Today, as I rushed to get a few things done before I drove to church to spend a few hours helping assemble reading glasses, I got overconfident and just believed I was pretty much fixed. My mind slipped and skipped gears when I was home alone only one hour between Phil leaving for work and me leaving for church. I am not ready to get things done at home alone. I need people around me to quiet my brain.

The two hours I spend around people will help me smooth the edges on the jack hammered rocks in my brain. I can't skip the step of healing and just jump into what needs to be done on the outside.

My rocks were rattling after a brief alone time where I did not take my illness seriously. I didn't pay attention to the importance of being mindful, of slowing my brain, of not drinking too much coffee, and focusing on my surroundings. I dazily loped around in my head and I began to feel it.

So, on my way to the beautiful church that is welcoming my donated time, I sanded my jagged rocks. I talked slowly to God about a simple thing. I want them smooth before I paint them. Talking to God feels like it takes some rough edges off my rocks.

It is nice driving alone sometimes. I can talk out loud when I pray. It removes the problem of wondering if I am in the right department of my brain when I think. When I pray lazily, I am thinking to my voices, not God. When I pray diligently, I am praying to God. When I'm tired of working on my brain in that way, I can pray out loud saying one of God's many names often to keep my focus pure.

By the time I arrived at church, my rocks weren't rattling as much. As I sand edges of lenses on the reading glasses that the missions department brings to people around the world, maybe I will get a rough corner or jagged edge off one or two of the rocks in my head.

Chapter 22
The End

I don't want to live on the edge of insanity. Do you? So, I sat and thought upon it for a time. No, I don't want to live on the edge of insanity.

How to end this book? Talk of 1000 years from now, floating on a cloud, letting God's love and joy completely in? Or, do I speak of Phil's loving friendship that pulled me back daily, into life, during my recovery as sickness pulled me to retreat? Or should I just say something I wrote in Pueblo State Hospital to myself? I think I know what it means now that I am not delusional:

Don't get mad (Insane), get even (Like the keel of a boat).

....and I ran out of words before I ran out of scars.